What Your
BODY
Is Telling You About Your
BUSINESS

The Key To Success Lies Within

Jennifer McCormack

What Your Body Is Telling You About Your Business: The Key To Success Lies Within. © Jennifer McCormack 2022

www.jennifermccormack.com.au

The moral rights of Jennifer McCormack to be identified as the author of this work have been asserted in accordance with the Copyright Act 1968

First published in Australia 2022 by Jennifer McCormack.

978-0-6455193-0-3

Any opinions expressed in this work are exclusively those of the author and are not necessarily the views held or endorsed by Jennifer McCormack.

All rights reserved. No part of this publication may be reproduced or transmitted by any means, electronic, photocopying or otherwise, without prior written permission of the author.

Disclaimer

All the information, techniques, skills and concepts contained within this publication are of the nature of general comment only, and are not in any way recommended as individual advice. The intent is to offer a variety of information to provide a wider range of choices now and in the future, recognising that we all have widely diverse circumstances and viewpoints. Should any reader choose to make use of the information herein, this is their decision, and the author and publisher(s) do not assume any responsibilities whatsoever under any conditions or circumstances. The author does not take responsibility for the business, financial, personal or other success, results or fulfilment upon the readers' decision to use this information. It is recommended that the reader obtain their own independent advice.

Dedication

To everyone that is ready to rise up from their challenges and stagnation into a place of flow, happiness and growth.

To my sons, Lachlan and Liam,

May you know yourself, love yourself and follow and live your dreams.

Table of Contents

Preface 1

Introduction 7

Part 1: 6 Governing Houses of the Ascension Pathway 43

    Introduction 45

    Life Force 51

    Life Path 63

    Business 77

    Finances 103

    Personal 113

    Health 125

Part 2: Reference Section—By Governing House 139

    Foundation 145

    Life Path 151

    Business 177

    Finances 193

    Personal 211

    Health 221

Part 3: Support **235**
    Tools 237
    Conclusion 239
    Resources 241
    Acknowledgements 243
    About The Author 245
    Index 247

Preface

I was struggling with business when I started writing this book. Financially, I was barely surviving. 90% of the people I worked with were not my ideal clients, but I did not mind. They brought in an income. I helped people earn a month's salary in a week, healed digestion disorders, helped people overcome pain and assisted developers in selling properties worth $1.5 million in a down market within 24 hours. Nonetheless, I was not happy and questioned my work and my ability to run or even build a business.

In the last four years, I have quit my business about four times. Yes, I threw in the towel several times because I felt like a total amateur. I felt like I chased after every single dollar I earned. It felt so hard. I did not understand how I could help others build their business while I was horrible at doing it myself. I seemed to understand the technical aspects. I was a great kinesiologist, but for some reason, I could not practice what I preached.

Every strategy I tried did not work. I spend hours marketing myself to what felt like a brick wall. Yes, I felt like I was marketing myself to a brick wall—like no one could hear me. While writing this book, I realised who I was. I was marketing myself to a brick wall, and that brick wall was me. I had built a wall around myself to protect myself so that I would not get hurt. This also meant that people found it hard to get in. I had to put in twice the effort to get one single client over the brick wall and work with them. It got exhausting eventually, and the telling signs were all around me.

I learnt to listen to my body again, physically and emotionally. I learnt to love myself for the first time, and instead of putting up a brick wall, I took them down and established healthy boundaries. I worked on letting go of past hurt, past guilt and past grief. Soon, there was nothing left to let go of from what I could see. I learnt that I could not do this alone and I needed support to dig deeper. These were the two, biggest realizations I made from this self-discovery process. I needed someone else to take a look at me, my blocks and my energy with fresh eyes. I did not get just one person; I built a team of people. If I wanted to be the best I could, I needed to surround myself with the best people I could find to guide me through this process. I did not have to search for them. They were already within my reach. All I had to do was ask. And so, the journey began—the journey to support myself while being open to receive support, beautifully aligned clients, money and the life balance I was always aiming for.

I learnt that I needed to love the business journey, not just the results. I needed to love the ups and downs, appreciate the unpredictable nature of the process, and create my own path. I had to change my perspective to experience the joy in small rewards, not just the big wins, because there will not always be big wins. I did not want my happiness to be anchored on outward validations; this would mean throwing myself into a big, emotional rollercoaster. Learning to love the process was a huge shift for me. It remains a significant lesson, even as I continue to evolve.

My initial intention for this book was for it to be a marketing tool — a glorified business card. A way to cement my authority in my industry. Boy, was I wrong. The journey of writing this book took me deeper into profound self-healing. It ended up being a personal healing process that dug deep into the layers of my subconscious mind, unearthing conscious beliefs I held about myself, the way I perceived others and the world around me.

This book revealed my insecurities about speaking my truth, sharing my message, and working with clients that I had previously perceived to be "better than me". I built this internal hierarchy system of who was better and more deserving than others, and I was definitely nowhere near the top of the list. Just another brick wall that I put up, another reason why the business was not allowed to be easy, another reason why I needed to work hard for money. The truth is, my self-worth was really low, and I felt like I did not deserve all that I wanted. I learnt that there is always a reason why we do not have what we want and that on some level, it comes down to being deserving of it or not.

This book was a huge healing and transformative process for me. It helped me expand my business vision beyond my family, my clients (past, present and future clients) and me. Yes, I want to help impact people's lives, but I also want them to impact others. I have always loved the idea of the butterfly effect. It also helped me gain confidence in myself (this self-confidence still grows till date) and my abilities, to the extent that I feel comfortable within myself. I learnt to market myself and my services even with the knowledge that I may get potential criticism. Through this and much more, the number of patients I work with has increased. The quality of my clients has improved and my revenue has more than tripled.

This is my exact intention for you. To allow the words on these pages uplift you and subject your inner wounds to healing. To expand your awareness and empower you to transcend your life by living it out authentically with a vision and purpose far greater than yourself.

It is time for we entrepreneurs to understand that there is no separation between us and our business, which means the stresses, anxieties, beliefs and values that surround our personal lives manifest in our businesses as well.

After years of working with the Chinese Five Elements philosophy and working with business owners, I have noticed certain behavioural patterns and outcomes. By pulling all this information together, I developed the Business Ascension Model. The Business Ascension Model evaluates mental and physical stresses (both on a muscle and organ level) and identifies how pain and discomfort correlate to the results we experience (or the results we do not experience) in our lives and businesses. In other words, our being is a pure reflection of our outcomes, but also a reflection of the results we will achieve in the future. If you want to change your future, you need to change the person you are right now. I call this the conscious creation mode.

By learning and flowing with this model, you will learn to understand a great deal about yourself and understand how a new awareness can heal you physically and mentally. You will observe an overall shift in life itself, evident in the nature of results you obtain.

I invite you, through this book, to let go and dig deeper into yourself and discover your own inner healing. I invite you to achieve greatness in your life and business.

Introduction

Many people that walk into my clinic are exhausted and overwhelmed. They are mentally and physically tired and do not know the next steps to take. All they want is an amazing life for themselves and their loved ones. Instead, the feel unaccomplished—like a failure.

They are striving for the ultimate freedom that entrepreneurship perceives to offer and want to be the best version of themselves in the process. Instead, they feel unsupported, drained and on the edge of burnout.

They work so hard and people around them can see that. They can also see the short fuse, frustration, and long hours. While they want you to give up the dream, all you want is to feel supported in your goals. Not feeling heard and understood can leave you feeling lonely and even abandoned in your endeavour to pursue your true purpose.

It is not that you are bad at what you do. In fact, you are most likely up there with the best. It is not even about having a good strategy; strategy is only 30% of the equation.

I want to help you uncover the other 70%. The self-belief, the self-love, the enthusiasm, the balance and love for yourself and your path, to the point that it does not matter who is with you on your journey. It does not matter who is supporting you or who is not, because you are so focused and support yourself on your path. You deeply and unconditionally believe with every inch of your being that you have everything you need to get through this stage and thrive in the direction of your dreams, in trusting that the people, event and knowledge that you require for your journey will attract to you at the right time. That you are 100% in alignment with your dreams and goals. You can empower your mind, body and soul to execute that strategy with ease and flow.

That person you dream of being, you are already them. Yes, that is right. That person is already you. Only beliefs stand in the way of seeing who you truly are, what you are made of and what you can achieve. Somewhere on this journey we have put ourselves into human cage of limited potential never realising that the cage was never locked.

You not only have all the tools and resources that you require, but you also have an internal GPS as well. An emotional guidance system that allows you to feel when you are out of alignment with your souls' purpose. When out of alignment, you are not broken or missing anything. You are simply tolerating an emotional state that does not feel good.

The frustration, the anger, the resentment, the guilt and lack of self-worth—all these are your emotional indicators that tell you a shift needs to occur to realign you with your purpose. There are three kinds of shifts: shift in perspective, shift in acceptance and shift in action. When we hold onto discomforts, they become chronic emotions and finally manifest into physical discomfort and dis-ease.

This book will show you how to work backwards. You will learn to unravel the emotions, thoughts and feelings behind your physical pain. When we make it a priority to feel good, we not only allow emotional healing to occur, but also physical healing. In this letting go process, we allow ourselves to come into alignment with ease and flow, in our minds, bodies, businesses, and everything else we want to achieve in life.

You were born as a complete, perfect being for your journey of life.

That vision of freedom you are after is already yours. That vision of you capable of making a massive impact in this world is present, right here and right now ready for you to claim.

If you can dream it, you can achieve it.

If you can dream it, you can achieve it. These ideas do not come to you by chance. They are purpose-filled inspirations that come to YOU, because you can achieve them.

There are many things we never learnt about ourselves while growing up. We only start to gain insight into them as we start to question our reality, the direction we are headed and the world around us. Things become clearer when we question why we are not able to achieve what we desire, why we have what we have, and why people do the things they do. Why do we feel the way we feel? The path to clarity begins with the search for answers.

You are much more than your physical bodies, and my intention here is to help you see your body as a doorway back to your true essence. To learn to trust your innate wisdom that guides you forward, by listening to your emotional and physical responses to the happenings in your life. To see how the mind, body and soul work together to shape both our internal and external realities, which include our health, business, career and achievements.

You have the power to be, do and have anything you want. ANYTHING. You need to know who you are at your core, what you are capable of as a human being, and learn to take that internal guidance down your unique path. Respond to life with love, abundance, grace, ease and flow. This is what I want for you.

We need to relearn how to work with our emotions—how to lead a life of amazing opportunities and adventures. We need to learn how to love ourselves again.

We did not come here to suffer and put up with just feeling 'ok'. We came here to create and thrive. The so-called sufferings are red flags for us to pay attention to along the way and an doorway of learning and growth back to our authentic self.

Through all of this, we can live a life of abundance and bring others into the light of endless possibilities just by being our real self. We can teach the younger generation, our peers, partners, family and community how to get back in touch with themselves, to listen to their mind, body and soul.

Change is possible. A negative emotional state does not have to last forever. Your feelings do not have to be a by-product of how others treat you or the events of your life. We are the drivers of our own destiny. How we think, feel and act—who we are and what we wish to create—is in our hands.

These emotions we hold on to have a direct impact on the quality of our lives. They consume our being and affect the results we achieve within our businesses. I believe that business owners are like strategically placed role models around the world, and when we are about to build a business, it is no different from building and creating our lives. We are responsible for the message we spread to our consumers. Are you spreading a message of love, health and wealth or a message of lack and fear?

This book may just be your 'go-to' guide in business and life. I have designed it to be an easy read and reference. I suggest you read part 1 fully, to understand the concept of how the body, mind and soul work so beautiful together and help shape the reality of our business, health and wellbeing.

This book is in a strategic order for you; it starts from your foundation and works its way up. Looking at life this way helps us to understand our actions and intentions and provides a framework for the next phase.

A quote stuck with me from the book 'A Man's Search for Meaning' is: A man who has a solid why, can withstand almost any how.

Understanding who we are, what we want from life and why we want it, gives us a solid foundation to build on. We can go one step further, which is knowing how we will feel once we have achieved our dreams. Feelings and emotions are the number 1 key to achieving anything.

Many business owners focus on sales results and finances. However, using this model that I have laid out for you, we learn that money is a by-product of serving our ideal customer from our zone of genius. In other words, when we know who we are and what difference we want to make in the world, we spread our message with authenticity and connect with those who need to hear it. The by-product of this in the business world is sales. It is never the main focus (although we need to have goals and fully understand our finances). Our focus needs to be on service. We will delve deeper into this later.

Part 2 is your 'go-to' reference guide. Here, you can look up your muscular physical discomforts and understand why you are experiencing the pain and discomfort in that area and what to do about it. You will learn about what emotions are stored in those muscles. We always feel emotions before physical pain. However, we are all different. Some of us will notice the physical discomfort first because a lot of our emotional feelings have been subdued or blocked out.

Here, you will find practical advice on your business strategy as well as some self-assessment questions to foster new awareness of yourself and your situation. Many times, through awareness, the shifts can occur, old stories are let go of, new flow begins, and pain is released.

As I shared in the Preface of this book, just by writing this book and raising my awareness to how my own body, mind and soul were reacting to the way my world and business was at the time, I saw profound shifts in my personal life and the results I was having in my business. I want this book to not only give you the understanding of how to elevate your business but to also help you obtain better balance, health and wealth in your life.

It is time to go forth and create your dream life.

Foundation Principle

You are perfect and complete; you are beautiful inside out. You are exactly where you are meant to be.

Your current position is the right place to move forward from. Even when you are experiencing struggle and discomfort, believe that you are at the appropriate place in the time of your life. Sometimes, we feel stuck in our minds, stuck in our bodies and stuck on our path. The truth is, nothing is missing. We have just become a little disconnected from ourselves. We have paid too much attention to other people's opinions, the news, social media and automatically living by subconcious beliefs that do not serve our higher purpose. When we are disconnected, our soul tries to whisper directions on how to return home. It does this through our intuition, emotional pain, physical pain, and lastly, through the discomforts that we experience in our daily lives.

Many of us see our lives from a physical perspective. We see people around us as bodies with brains. We see houses, cars, clothes, beaches, lakes and money. However, what we are experiencing through our eyes is only .001% of reality. Yes, you read that right. What we think is real is only a small fraction of what reality actually is.

When we look at what makes up a physical object, including ourselves, we see cells, particles, and the atoms that make up those particles. We can break these down even further to the electron, protons and neutrons, which are the building blocks of an atom. Science tells us that we are made up of atoms, but an atom in itself is .001% matter and 99.999% energy.

Quantum physics suggests that the energy of an object is influenced and can be altered by the energy of another object within its proximity.

This is why proximity is power. The five people we spend the most time with influence our essence and personality. Generally, we all affect one another's energy field, both positively and negatively. We can be the biggest source of motivation and encourangement or our energy can be pulled down by the people around us.

What we also know is that when energy is in motion, we humans experienced this as E-motions. To define our reality and bring anything into physical manifestation, it needs to be felt emotionally first. These emotions will attract the objects and experiences into your reality.

How do you change your emotions and incorporate your desires into your reality?

Your emotions are rooted in the way you think. Your persecption of events in your life shape your thinking process by developing belief systems that control your subconscious, hence, your current experience. In addition, your circle, actions, how you see yourself individually and in comparison to others, reflect these thought pattern. These are some of the building blocks of our conscious and subconscious minds. Our noticeable thoughts account for approximately 5 % of our mind.

The remaining 95% of your mind is the many layers of your subconscious. Your beliefs, habits, values, past experiences, past hurts, past pain, past loves and sabotage programs consititute your subconscious mind, which functions on autopilot. The questions is, does your subconsious programming bring you closer to your dreams or further way?

Before I became a Kinesiologist, I was a fashion designer for 17 years. As a fashion designer, I thought I needed to work hard, long hours to get noticed by my colleagues and managers, secure my annual raise and feel involved—like I was actually making substantial contribution. I used to work 10 – 12 hours daily. Yes, they noticed. Yes, I got the recognition, and yes, I got my annual raise every year. This proved my belief that I needed to work extra hard to make money. Eventually, I burnt out and quit the industry all together. There were so many redflags along the way, showing me that my actions were not right for me. The anger and frustration I constantly felt. The stomach aches. The back aches—I spent years with upper back pain. My back pain was telling me I was going down the wrong path. I was a good designer. Soon enough, I progressed to managering, which I executed dexterously but hated every bit of it. It was not me. It took me off my desired path. This was my outer world telling me that I was not only disconnected from my intuition, but also what to do with my career and I never questioned it.

When we believe something, we desperately search for evidence to prove that what we believe is true. I never asked myself if managing made me happy. It was something I believed to be the natural progression from what I saw of others and what was expected of me.

Foundation Principle

Most of our beliefs are constructed before we are seven years old. These are the years our subconious is open ready to soak in all our experinces. We also soak in beliefs, values and traits from people around us without questioning them.

I watched my dad work a lot, but then we had what we needed. This was what I observed from my perspective as a young girl anyway. I connected working hard with getting what I needed. This is a typical example of how the subconscious mind functions on autopilot.

When we start to recongise and understand these discomforts, our perception starts to shift, so does our energy and the world around us. These happen so that you can see what you are meant to see to be able to heal. When I had these shifts, I started connecting with people that created their ideal life on their own terms. People that had already adopted the idea of conscious existence. This was the confirmation that I needed to know it was also possible for me.

The mind-body-soul is such an amazing trio. When we learn to listen, connect, understand and work with them the most extraordinary things occur. The truth is, as you sit here and read this book, you have no idea just how powerful you are. Most of us do not know, and even after a decade of self-discovery and personal development, I know there are many things about myself that I still do not know. The same goes for you. Know that the world—your world—externally and internally, is a place of infinite expansion. I get excited when I think about the endless possibilities that are still yet to discover.

Our mind, body and soul are three of many parts of us that I want to discuss in this book. I see these as the conscious driving forces of our physical existence that we call life. We are not physical beings having a spiritual experience but spiritual beings having a physical experience. This means that we are and have always been one with the universe. As God mentions in the bible, His power is in everyone and everything on earth. The trees, the birds—all living creatures, great and small. What you see and know the universe to be at its purest form is exactly who you are.

The mind can adopt certain values and beliefs that mask our true nature. This book is designed to bring you one step closer to the universal source energy that defines you. Through this connection, you will have an authentic life experience. You will learn to enjoy the adventure, the contrasting experiences and the people life has to offer. You will not only survive but also thrive in life and in your business.

The mental health, emotional intelligence and spiritual expansion journey help us expand into our greatness. This was the journey originally designed for us before we learnt that the expectations of society are a greater force than our own expectation. We care so much about what people say, what the government says, what our teachers say—their opinions overshadow our internal connection and truth.

As we are an extension of source energy/God/Universe (whichever you are most comfortable with), we can create, attract and be anything we want to be. From this pure standpoint, there are no limits, no negative or positive; there is only pure love and experiences. Here, our imaginations is boundless and our knowledge is limitless.

We have a mind to help us along this journey—a choose-your-own-adventure, where we are exposed to the great contrasts of this world. The perceived good and bad, black and white, love and fear, intimacy and envy help us choose our path, the path that feels right for us. How do we know what love is if we have not experienced fear, betrayal or hate? How do we know we want to experience love if we have nothing to compare it to? Every experience provides a benchmark for the next.

Every experience is neither good nor bad. Our personal perceptions of these experiences determine what is 'good' or 'bad'. For a person that believes they need to work hard to make money, on some level, this belief works for them. It validates their hard work.

The child of such a person may grow up craving their parent's attention and wanting their love so much because they were never at home. For the child, this can then trigger the formation of beliefs around money, work and receiving love. It is important to note that every individual perceives events and situations differently. Just because you consider something as negative does not mean everyone else sees it in that same light.

It is important for the progression of your journey that your grip on your beliefs are not too tight or rigid. One day, these belief systems will be challenged when they no longer serve you. They will lose their relevance in your life. At this point, you will grow through them and have to let go and recreate new belief systems for the next chaper of your life.

The truth is that every chapter of your life requires a different version of you. You get to decide who you are and who you are willing to become. If you want more ease, flow, and abundance in your life, you will need to break down the resistances that come up along the way. You want a path with the least resistance but that wont come naturally unless you are preconditioned with beliefs that support you along that path. Choose the path that feels right, not the path that feels familiar. We are faced with familiarity when past thoughts and feelings resurface. Unearthing new chapters and new versions of ourselves will not be a familiar feeling. It may even be extremely uncomfortable.

On a chemical level, the feeling of anxiety and that of a breakthrough have the same chemical structure. This is why it is important to allow yourself space to become centred within your body and mind so you can tell the difference and evolve. You can do this by bringing in to your daily routine a reflective practice. A space and time where you can reflect back on the thoughts, feeling and actions from the day from that grounded perspective. A reflective practice also enables us to catch those self sabotaging thoughts and beliefs quicker, instead of allowing them to run our days, weeks and even years.

Our minds and emotions help us navigate through that personal journey. Your emotions are an internal GPS that can help guide you on that path of least resistance. When we experience love and joy, our internal guidance system is letting us know that we are on the right path. As you keep moving in that direction, you will attract more of what feels good, in line with the energy you are projecting. One of the most powerful universal laws is that you attract what you give, no exceptions.

As you are travelling along this path it is natural that not every day will be smooth sailing. There will be ups and theire will be downs. Many of us sit in this stuck spot for too long and even start to question your path at this time. Know that the downs are your internal GPS indicating to you that there is a belief or internal program blocking your path that you need to work through. This is your higher self giving you another opportunity to grow and uplevel.

Most of us have never learnt to trust ourselves and listen to the way we feel, mentally or physically—to look for answers and guidance from within. Some of us have been taught to ignore our feelings and suppress them, to get on with life.

When a child is upset, many parents distract them to stop them from crying or throwing a tantrum. They feel that this is the best approach for them. This is a classic example of society not allowing us to experience the full gamet of our emotions, and therefore end up being stuck in our bodies to be triggered later in life.

You may have learnt that it is forbidden or uncomfortable to others for you to show your love, anger, and grief to the world. Anger is not a socially acceptable emotion for women to express, so we learn to suppress it. Anger is suppressed in the liver and can start to breed resentment and unhappiness. We learn to disconnect from our emotions and therefore ourselves and lose our sense of identity, after which one of the biggest side effects is a absence of self-love and self-trust set in. Inturn, we start to seek external validation and this is where women can unexpectantly end up in controlling relationships.

For a lot of men, it is not acceptable to show love, vulnerability, and heartache; it is more acceptable to show anger. Men are meant to be the strong protectors that provide for the family. Through the shutting down of their emotional state, anger arises because it is what they feel comfortable with expressing. Through this, a lot of us have learnt to look at external sources for answers. We are taught to please our parents, to adhere to the structure and teachings of the education system, we learn that all the answers are found externally, so we do not even think that WE have the answers to OUR questions. We end up questioning our own internal voice. I ask you this: Why would anyone else have the answers to your personal questions? When you learn to listen to yourself, learn who you are again, and learn to unconditionally love and trust yourself (because you once did), life will show you the love that it has to offer and oh boy, it is so beautiful. So much clarity, peace of mind and inspiration will flow to you like a river of abundance.

Do not despair if you've never travelled the path within. The path has always been there and it can once again be dusted off and travelled upon. We are given a lifetime to experience this journey and the contrast of your past adventurs will become the perfect bench mark to start living a conscious life and bring forth your inner desires into the world.

There are many routes to the same diestination, so do not despair if you feel way off course at the moment. Where you are now is the perfect place to start, and you can get anywhere is life from this place. Remembering you are always one decition away from a very different life and every hurdle we face is another opportunity to grow. There is no right or wrong way, just the one that FEELS right and light for YOU.

Many entrepreneurs start their business as a side hustle while still working their 9 – 5 job. I often see them start resenting their job when they feel it becomes a distraction from them building their own business. I often hear them say, 'All my GOOD hours are being "used up" working for someone else, and I do not even want to be there. There is no future there for me'.

We know from the universal laws that resentment breeds more resentment and life will show us more reasons to resent our work and you will even start resenting other things and people in your life.

There are three ways to change our circumstances;

The first is to change it. To walk away, to make a physical change.

The second is acceptance. This is especially important when dealing with other people. We cannot change people. In the face of confrontation, we may need to accept that disagreements are bound to happen. From there, you can decide the best action to take. I find in my practice that one of the hardest lessons for people to learn is accepting that we cannot change people. We need to learn to acknowledge that they are on their own path, one which is neither right nor wrong, but different from ours. When we accept people as they are, it fosters internal calmness.

The final way is to change your perspective. While this is not an easy way, it can be the most rewarding and fulfilling. When we learn to change our perspective, it not only liberates us from the current problem, but it also has a flow on effect in other areas of our life.

Another way to change your perspective is to come from a place of gratitude. What is it giving me?

- It is providing you with an income while you build your business.
- It can help you grow your knowledge base for your own business.
- You may love the people interaction that it provides.
- It enables you to make mistakes without personally wearing the costs.
- It is taking the pressure off your business to provide financially, so you can set up the foundations for long-term success.

The most crucial part is that it is taking the pressure off your business to perform. I see this a lot when there is so much pressure on a business to provide. It leads to the owners lacking clarity, long term vision, and long term growth strategies and puts them in a scarcity mindset. They are stressed from trying to survive, as they are looking at short term strategies and solutions to put food on the table. They execute strageties that are not aligned to them and onboarding clients they don't like, simply to bring in a dollar, any dollar. Just remember, you did not come here to 'just survive'; you came here to thrive.

Taking the time to execute from alignment is a crucial point for long term growth and being able to personally sustain that growth without heading in the direction of burnout. There is two parts to alignment here, one is of being in alignment emotionally and energetically and also with the strategy. Not all strategies are going to be right for you right now, just as much as having resistance to execute the nesecary strageties to grow your business.

I remember having an internal struggle working with clients that earned more money than me. I had no problems working with start ups and others whom I perceived to earn less than me, but for everyone else I didn't feel skilled enough, good enough and lost a lot of my confidencce. One morning, on coming out of mediation, an epiphany came over me. When I looked at my clients, no matter what a person's income was, the problems they had externally and internally were all very similar. The way their bodies responded to problem was the same. Their back was always sore when they did not have clarity about where they were headed. Thyroid problems presented when they were consistently afraid to speak out. The reason they were coming to me is that I had the knowledge and tools in this area to help them. In fact, I found that, the more comfortable I got, the more I raised my prices and the more I attracted clients that were dedicated to healing journey. I was attracting less people that saw themselves as 'victims'. Rather, they took ownership of their journey and saw it as such an empowering process.

There are three ways to gain clarity:

1. **Direct from source energy/universe/God. Prayer is the vehcial in which we ask a question, while meditation downloads the answers and clarity.**
2. **Through our emotions. How do you feel? Do you feel in flow or can you feel the resistant emotions rise?**
3. **Through our physicality. This is the pain and discomforts of your body compared to the energised balanced state.**

This book will help you look at your physicality and your emotions to understand what is triggering these pains and emotions. While you embark on this journey, your intuition will become louder as a byproduct. What you will discover is that the core root of the pain and discomfort was the messages your intuitions was trying to give you all along.

Traditional Chinese Medicine suggests that our thoughts have a direct impact on the way we feel physically. Every emotions that we feel is connected to our energy, our muscles, organs and sytems of the body. Even modern-day science is catching up with this.

Have you ever been on a first date and had butterflies in your stomach? There are no butterflies in there; it is merely a chemical reaction that is occuring. Our thoughts and feelings release what we call neuropeptides. The role of these peptides is to activate certain chemicals in different parts of our body. When we are happy and in love, hormones like oxytocin and serotonin are released in the body. In the same way, anger causes adrenaline to release. And stress and anxiety release cortisol.

The aim of these is to help us physically cope while we process our emotions and bring the body back into homeostatis. Good thoughts help us sustain that homeostasis (balance within the mind, body, and soul). Not fully processing your emotions and holding onto thoughts that do not feel good for a prolonged period, can overloaded the body, and a chemical imbalance in the system starts to occur. This imbalance causes discomfort and dis-ease within the body. When we take this one step further, there are different emotions that reside and put pressure on different organs and muscles within the body.

The dis-ease and dis-comforts that we feel on a physical level are all connected with thoughts, feelings, and emotional imbalances that we currently hold on a conscious or subconscious level. This can be an imbalance in our belief system, a belief that no longer works for us or a emotions that we haven't fully felt through. The 'I need to work hard for money' belief, and the 'I need to be a present parent' belief can be conflicting. Your emotions will tell you this through, the guilt and shame that rise. If we ignore the discomforts we feel, eventually, it will manifest in our physical body. We can ease the pain by changing our thoughts, emotions, feelings and internal programs.

Over the years, I have been working with business owners to follow patterns and cycles that have been present in the Chinese Five Element system and relate them back into the entrepreneurial world. From this, I developed the ascension model that helps you and your business thrive and attain mental, physical, emotional and spiritual balance. You can have a beautiful, purposeful life, not just for now but forever.

Business Cycle

As entrepreneurs, you need a solid foundation to build a successful, thriving business. You develop a business plan required to pave a clear, strategic path you envision for yourself. You write down your goals that you really want to achieve. You pour your heart, soul, and time into planning the business, almost never considersing the other 80% of the pie. Strategy is only 20%. Even when you have a solid business andmarketing plan and mentors, you can struggle and even fail, unless your beliefs are aligned with your goals and you believe you can execute them.

Some years ago, I worked with Sandra (her name has been changed due to privacy reasons). Sandra was a Business Coach, who helped people build and scale their businesses. She was going through a bit of a rought spot when she approached me—deep in debt and borrowing money from friends to afford basic neccesities. She felt overwhelmed, mentally and physically exhausted, disconnected and therefore, lost belief in herself and her abilities. Next, she was going to have to get a part-time job. It is important to note that she was a great coach with a tested and proven business strategy and marketing plan. When I asked her what her goal was for the next month, she said $10,000 was exactly what she needed to get out of debt and to help her move forward.

Over the next four weeks, we did a lot work together. We tapped into emotions stored within the body, beliefs that no longer worked for her, and destructive ancentral patterns that were holding her back . I empowered her with knowledge of how to nuture herself and construct meaningful routines to set up her day. By the end of the month, she was realigned, happier, and more confident. In the final session she mentioned that she reached her goal and was absolutely stocked with the result. This was the shift and realignment required to generate energy flow and momentum in her business. I want to remind you that she did not change her business strategy but did internal work instead. We shifted engrained beliefs that she had to work extremely hard to attain success. Her father said she would never successfully run her own business—that she was better off working a 9-5. All this needed to be shifted.

Some of our beliefs we consciously know, while some are hidden out of sight, but still run on auto pilot.

There are many other ways to show that strategy and market conditions alone will not make your business thrive or fail. I believe a business can rise or fall in any market condition. History shows us this several times. Consider Sir Richard Branson, Steve Jobs, and Warren Buffet. As I write this book, we are in the middle of the COVID-19 pandemic. All my clients that have been commited to doing the inner work continue to run healthy businesses. Some sailed along as usual, while others have shifted online due to restrictions. The COVID-19 pandemic and its associated occurrences reinforced the benefits of doing this inner work for outter results was far more effective than just looking at strategy alone.

Destructive Cycle of Business

There are two sides of every coin. Just as there is a path that leads to business growth and life balance, there are also destructive cycles. Destructive cycles symbolize disconnection and imbalance. Here, you lose touch with your essence and inner being, the times when you listen more to things in your external environment and become out of touch with your own intuition and desires, focusing only on external results. Simple daily tasks can begin to feel heavy, overwhelming, and tiring. This is when things can start to spiral out of control.

I observe destructive cycles in women who are in the phase of reconnecting with themselves when their kids start school. For so long, they have been focused on raising the children and supporting their partners' in their careers. They had become preoccupied with pleasing everyone else that they forget how to put themselves first. They forget who they are, what they want and ultimately deviate from their path, and lose sight of their life ambitions.

It is easy for this loss of purpose to occur in business, when you are overly focused on the finiances rather than why you started your business and your customer. Since the late 1970s, there has been a drastic shift in focus from leading people and upholding legacies to pleasing the stake holders and keeping a perfect balance sheet, hence, more profit-oriented business. Essentially, finance should be a secondary goal in business. When made the primary focus, passion and purpose is lost, the business foundation is threatened, and your customers ends up feeling like just another number.

This is not just a pattern for mothers; it can happen to any of us because we fail to connect with ourselves to discover what drives our happiness. What does make you happy? What do you want? What do you want to achieve? If we don't ask these sort of questions, we end up unconsciusly treading down someone else's path, leading to physical and emotional manifestations of derailment.

Like a lot of things in life, these destructive cycles have patterns. By learning how to identify these patterns as they come up, we can pick ourselves up and get back on our path. Life is a mirror; it will always reflect back at you your blocks and barriers. You just need to check in with yourself and listen for the answers.

A business may fail to thrive because it lacks the nurturing and support around the fundamentals of business. You need to grow a business from a solid foundation. We may have a well thought out business strategy, but this is only 20% of the equation. The other 80% is our mindset, heartset, health, and energy. Is this in alignment with where you want to take the business? We must nuture our self-awareness to notice when we have deviated, this way, we can notice when it's likely that we are off course and to stop, correct, and realign. We can not do this head deep in strategy or from an egocentric place.

Whenever I work with entrepreneurs, we work on beliefs, values, emotions, and energetic blocks rather than strategy or skill level. Aligning these aspects of us strengthens the current strategy and gives us new awareness and perspective to evolve and gain new strategies that are more aligned with where we want to go.

The people we wish to serve, how we are going to serve them, communicate with them, and how much we are going to charge them are such small components of the bigger picture.

We cannot charge correctly for our products and services if we have deep self-worth issues. We will undercharge and our audience will not see the value in what we are offering because we do not see value within ourselves.

If we do not feel like we know enough, we will always feel inferior in some way and that will project outwards. We need to learn to notice how we talk to ourselfs in our head and be kind to ourselves. We need to nurture our business from within.

We all run subconscious paradigms that can either contribute to or sabotage our growth. Many women I have worked with believe that we live in a man's world; they struggle to find their place in the business arena. This is because they run a sabotage program that says, 'I cannot be a successful business owner because I am a woman or mother'.

These sabatoage programs are rooted in our pasts, especially our childhood. If you feel like you have been put down, abandoned, or rejected as a child, you may find marketing extrememly difficult because deep down, you do not feel accepted, listened to, or worthy. As an adult these programs extend beyond the impact from our parent and influence all relationships in our life. This will also impact your service fees. Even with the best marketing copy or the most perfect price structure, unfortunately energy doesn't lie and you may end up attracting people that do not see the value in you, do not apprieciate your product or service, and will think you are too expensive (even if you charge a low price).

The 'destructive cycle' indicates a need for clarity on how to prevent problems in business. If you feel that you are struggling with an aspect of business, this will give you an insight into what may be going on within, resulting in your current results.

This is the time to be honest with yourself to see where the problem lies. Are you struggling with cash flow because of money beliefs, or are you not offering the right products/services to your client? Are you connecting with your ideal client through your messaging?

Let us look at the cycle itself, starting with the business element.

If you struggle with marketing and communications, connecting with ideal clients, setting 'acceptable' fees, or reaching financial goals, you need to check the 'Life Path' element for balance. If imbalance is detected in these areas, the next step is to determine the root cause. Do you need a break to recharge your purpose and reignite your inspiration? Have you structured your business to have balance—to have the lifestyle you are after? Do you have passion and purpose?

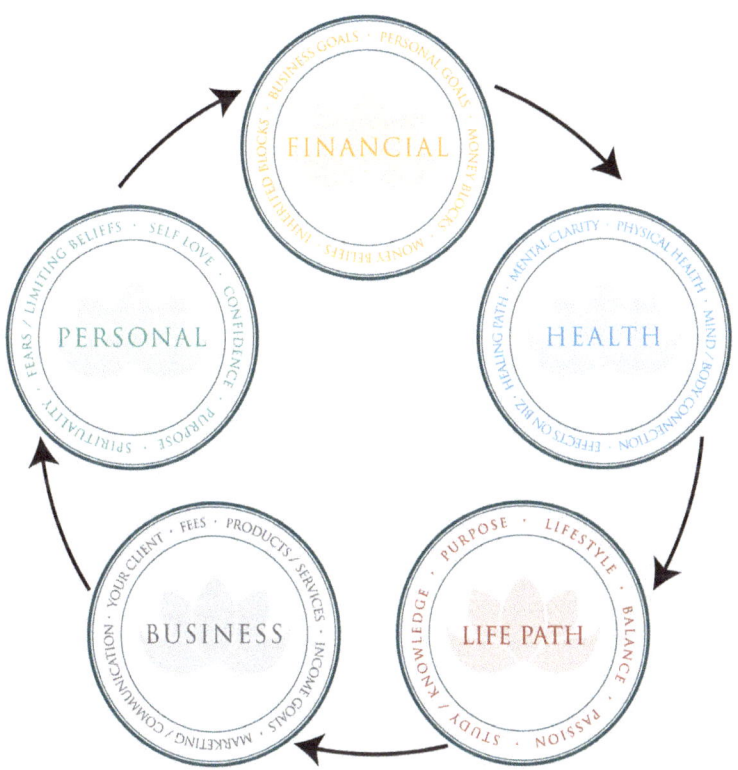

Does your purpose match your passion? Do you need to gain extra knowledge or study?

If the Life Path element is not balanced, study the 'Health' element. How is your mental/physical health? Are you always stressed, overwhelmed, or anxious? Are you listening to your self and your body, or are you constantly listening to others? Seeking external validation and advice? What emotions keep rising that you keep pushing side? Are you nourishing yourself the right way for you? What is your body trying to tell you?

If there is an imbalance in the Health element, check the 'Financial' element. What are your conscious and subconscious programming and beliefs around money, savings, budgeting, and setting financial goals? Do they work for you or against you? What did you learn from your parents around money and wealth? Are you focusing too much on the finances to your bodies detriment?

Study the 'Personal' element if you feel there is an imbalance in the Financial element. Are you nurturing yourself? Are you holding yourself back? Are you giving yourself unconditional love? Or are you constantly putting other first and living from a empty cup? Are you living your life to please others? Discover what fulfils you in life. Think of the nearest future; one month, six months, next year, what does this look like if it was aligned to your deepst calling?

If you are totally overwhelmed and feeling any imbalances mentally or physically, it is time to take a different approach—an approach you resonate with on a deeper level. One that encompasses your mental, emotional, physical, and spiritual life and connects you to the greater purpose that you are already a part of. This is the Ascension Path.

The ascension path is about igniting and aligning your true self from the inside out. We are spiritual beings having a human experience. After we are born, we tend to forget who we are and what we are capable of. We enter this world as beautiful, little sponges ready to absorb all the love and adventure it has to offer. We absorb other people's love and nurtutring but also their fears, beliefs, and values along

Destructive Cycle of Business

Ascension Path

37

the way. We mimick how they see the world and how they compare themselves to others.

The belief from Dad that we need to work hard and long hours to make ends meet. The belief from mum that women are unsupported by corporate environments. The beliefs from our school, coaches, friends, mentors, basically everyone that helps nuture and mentor us along the way.

Our work here is not to fix ourselves; you are not broken. Our duty is to unlearn what we have been taught, reunite with our true selves, and live an authentic aligned life. We will discover that the previous beliefs and values were there for a reason. We believed they would keep us safe and secure in some way. As my awareness expanded, I saw how 'working hard for money' gave me drive, determination, and even some self-belief, but that was before it turned into anxiety and burnout, along with heightened anger and frustration. That is when most of us notice the need for change and to do the inner work to balance the mind, body, and soul is the perfect place to start.

There are always two sides to us; I call them the angel and the devil (sounds a little extreme, but you get the contrast). We determine which side of us gets fed the most by the choices we make. We can feed the angel by striving for balance and harmony. When we flow with our internal emotional guidance system and run values, beliefs and programs that work for us and not against us. This does not mean things will always be peachy and rosy, what it does do is it equips us to face the challenges when they do arise, to become more self-aware and a little less driven by ego and external influences.

Every belief, value, thought, and emotion in our head, in our hearts, and in our subconscious can be changed. We are NOT stuck with the same beliefs cycle forever. This is important to hear as a lot of people think that because they have experienced depression, anxiety, or back pain for a prolonged period of tme, that is is now part of who they are – a part of their identity forever. This could not be further from the truth. You now understand that if you are feeling discomfort mentally, emotionally or physically, it is rising to be released. It wants you to heal and let it go.

When you travel the ascension path, you will begin to notice the beliefs, sabotages, fears, and emotions that no longer serve you. They manifest as thoughts, feelings, emotions, or physical pain and through the awareness of your experiences. These present a chance to create new beliefs, propel forward, release the stress and pave a new way for growth.

With the ascension path, we learn to grow and experience life according to our true purpose. To walk authentically and fearlessly on our life's path, trusting the universe and our connection to it. The energy within and around us is here to guide and support you on this journey.

When we learn who we are at our core and understand that we are connected to the universe, we can feel that we are always supported on our life path; we have everything we need within us to thrive. We understand that all our problems are internal and everything external is a reflection of who we are on the inside. If one notices a lack of affection from their partner, one would say they are closed off, emotionless, or are not open to receive the love given to them. The question should be: 'Is there a part of me that is closed off to receiving love from my partner?', 'How can I learn to give myself a little more love?'

When we react to what others day or do, it is a trigger within us that is ignited. We very often sit in this place of discomfort for much longer than we need to. It is important to give yourself time to feel into what is happening and the reactions that it is conjuring up inside you. We often shy away from fully experiencing the feelings of the moment, but this is part of the emotional cycle of healing. From here you can begin to explore what may be deeper. Your questions may be: What did they trigger and why? From the space of knowing who we are and that we are always supported—that we have everything we need—we can look deeper into understanding ourself.

The ascension pathway teaches us to connect deeper with self, through which we will discover who we really are and what is our role in the universe. When we sit in our zone of genius, we learn to serve others from a place of love. This not only helps the community and those we serve, but also nourishes our hearts, our souls, and our back pocket. The by-product of living an authentic life in your own lane and serving the people you were born to serve, is that the energy exchange happens—in this age, we call this money.

The reason why we are in a plague of overwhelm and burnout is because for so long we have been taught to do things the other way around. To focus on money first and serving second. Money is a by-product not a primary goal.

This book will take you step-by-step on a journey through each governing house of the ascension path. You will learn what muscles, emotions, and experiences are related to each other. Through this, you will be able to identify the emotions and beliefs you need to let go of or the actions to take, which will empower you to lead a smoother, happier life and automatically manifest a new reality.

PART 1

6 Governing Houses of the Ascension Pathway

Introduction

Every successful venture requires a strategy to take you from where you are to where you want to go. Be it a vague or carefully thought out plan, it is easier to see a way forward when there is some sort of plan in place. This goes for both business and life. Where do you want to go? What do you wnt to create? How do you want to feel on your journey? These questions we have never been taught to ask ourselves, yet they give you so much clarity.

Clarity helps us to create a road map, it also helps us create boundaires for that road map. We are able to get clear on what we want in and what we don't want. This includes people, beliefs, actions, behaviours, jobs, absolutely everything.

I was in consultation with a 19-year-old guy a while back, whom was studying entrepreneurship at university. Initially, he believed he wanted to be an entrepreneur. Along the line, he lost motivation and did not know how the information in his course fit into the picture of entrepreneurship. I explained to him that I could understand why things did not seem to fit. The life pathways paved for us by the system has been done in such a way that we end up doing step three before step one and two, and then we wonder why we are confused and why university dropout rate is on the rise.

The ascension pathway that I take you through will show you that step one is about really getting to know ourselves from the core essence of who we authentically are, and through this understanding, we learn just how powerful we really are. We learn that we are not just a physical or emotional body. We learn the grand essence to life, our soul, which is connected to the universal energy. We are a spiritual being having a human exeperince.

Step two is about learning what we are here to do. What experiences do we want? In today's terms, what lifestyle do we want? What kind of people do we want to connect with? Where do we want to live? But the most important thing here is, how are we going to be of service to your community? What is our role here? Who am I here to serve, and how? Through this understanding, we can jump into step three, which is about the application, business, the act of service, and connecting with the people who we are to serve.

Today, a lot of people enter university barely knowing who they really are or where they want to be, hence why university for many doesn't resonate. We have a deep desire to know the 'why' behind things, and once we have paved the foundations of the first two governing houses, the knowledge we need to obtain through study has a solid 'why' attached to it. There is a line in the book, Mans Search for Meaning, which says: He who knows his 'why' for his existence will be able to bear almost any 'how.' In other words, when we have a goal or a dream that is connected to our purpose, the ebbs and flows in life are so much easier to navigate through, than a goal with no meaning.

When we move forward out of flow, our mind know this. We feel unmotivated and lost. When these feelings accumulate, they can turn into procrastination, anxiety, overwhelm and feel like we are not good enough. Our body also knows we are out of sequence and will respond to the thoughts and feeling of the mind. In this case, stomach issues, heartburn, food intolerances, asthma, bronchitis, and other physical manifestation of misalignment occur. Smoking can be a way to push these issues aside, acting as a smokescreen so we can keep moving forward and ignore the discord that is happening internally, as well as the triggered muscular pain, which I will take you through in Part two of this book.

This is because every thought we have, every belief we hold, whether it is conscious or unconscious, changes the internal chemistry of our body. The longer we hold the thoughts and beliefs that are not congruent with us, the stronger the pain and discomforts get, both mentally and physically, which also means the more disconnected we get from our soul.

Many of us have learnt to tolerate a certain level of pain and discomfort both mentally and physically. We have to relearn what it feels like to be pain-free again, what it feels like to operate at higher optimum energy levels, to be happy, content, in love, and to sit in a state of gratitude instead of a state of stress, despair, and survival.

I have divided this book into seven sections for you, which represent the six Governing Houses of life's ascension path. I have split the first Governing House into two sections, as they need to be embodied in a sequence before moving forward onto Governing House two. Each of these sections have their individual purpose in our lives and business, correlating with set of muscles, emotions, and meridian lines. These are all based on the five elements of philosophy outlined by Chinese Medicine.

Each of the six governing houses has its own set of muscles, organs, and emotions. I have listed these at the front of each section so that you can search by emotional or physical discomfort as a starting point. Some of us feel emotions a lot more, while others respond to what is happening to their physical body more. We all have different ways of connecting in, so I have made it easy for all of us.

Every mental and physical pain and discomfort we experience is our higher self trying to communicate with us. At first, it tries to connect through our intuition—our gut feeling—and when we are unable to receive these messages, it guides us through our emotions, always trying to bring us back to love. When we ignore these emotional signs, they manifest in the physical.

THE INSPIRATION YOU SEEK
IS ALREADY WITHIN YOU.
BE SILENT AND LISTEN.

—RUMI

LIFE FORCE

To build a successful and long-lasting business, we need to have a solid and well thought out foundation. But, when it comes to life and business, what does that mean?

It is time to gain a deeper sense of clarity by asking yourself these three questions:

1. Who am I?

2. What is my purpose here at the moment?

3. What does success look like to me?

This is a great time to create a forward 10 year plan for yourself, to help you move forward from this new found sense of purpose. It is time to really understand who we are at our core and just how much personal power we have. Some of us have been brought up in a world that makes us feel small. We believed that we were broken, that all the answers to our questions are ourside of us – claritiy that we need to search for instead of uncover from within. If you need more energy, you consume certain foods, take supplements, exercise, etc. If you are sad, you take antidepressants or go to the gym to ignite your endorphins. We have been taught more about quick fixes rather than healing for personal expansion.

When we realise we are complete beings, we learn to understand the immense power that we hold within us. The power to be, do, and have absolutely anything. The ability to turn our dreams into our realities.

From a basic standpoint, we are made up of the holy trinity, our mind, body, and soul. Our body and mind are impermanent as there is a beginning and an end to them. They come and go. Our soul is apart of the permanence of the universal energy.

As described in the book Conversations with God by Neale Donald Walshe, we are like a room in a house. The air in the house is from the same source, yet we are just one of its many rooms. There air in the kitchen is no different from the air in the master bedroom or the air in the lounge room. It just has a different external representation. US. In other words, each of us is the same at our core. We are just housed in different physical bodies and raised in different cultures with different values, beliefs, and experiences. The reason it is so important to remember this is that it fosters more compassion and understanding with other people and ourselves. There is no right or wrong belief, just beliefs that either work for us or don't.

Some of us believe in the universe; some of us believe in God, Source Energy, Allah, Jehovah, etc. The truth is not concerened with which faith is right or wrong; it is concerned with which faith is right for you. This is a questions that only you can answer.

The connection we have to the universe never goes away; it is our main guidance system. Sometimes, we silence it with the noise of the outer world and the mountain of thoughts in our minds. The main objective our soul provides for us, while we are experiencing this physical human life, is to maintain our life path. It does this by continually guiding us back to pure love, first through our intuitive thoughts, then through our emotions, and finally through our manifested physical pain and discomforts.

Why is it so important to be aware of our mind, body, and soul? Some of us run through life purely on a physical level and never really intently connect into our soul, by doing this you deny your gift of true unlimited power.

When we do feel broke, and experience on going fatigue, anxiety and sadness it is because we are pleasing others instead of ourseleves. Whether that be our family, spouce, our society or culture. You need to put you and your needs and wants first and then, only then will you gain all the answers you need along your journey.

Abundance

When we look at our physical body, we can see it is made up of 1% matter and 99% energy, the energy component being what binds the matter together. This energy not only allows our physical body to function, our minds to tick and our emotions to help us feel, but this energy is our life force. It filters down from the universal energy and makes up our physicality and our minds, direct from our soul.

When we begin to look at life from the lens of our soul, we learn to understand who we are. We are perfect beings, and everything we say and do is from a place of unconditional love. We have access to everything we need internally, like the answers to our question, direction, clarity, loving state of being, and contentment. This balanced internal world will attract an external world that matches it, through resources, people and experiences, health, and wealth. When we move forward from our soul, we are in a balanced state. This does not mean that we do not encounter stress. It means we are more equipped to work through stress with more ease .

If you experience anxiety or overwhelm and do not understand how to navigate through the cycle of those feelings, it will eventually manifest as physical pain or discomfort. When we experience joy and love, these will also manifest physically through good health, balance, wellbeing, and abundance. In any state of being, our internal worlds mimics our external reality. Our energy acts like a magnet; it brings more of what we are and think towards us. Many entrepreneurs in the initial stages, we are focused on the money they are or are not bringing in which puts a lot of pressure on themselves and their business. By focusing your time and energy on the lack of money, you attract a lack of money into your experience and will consistently see evidence on why it is not coming in; like not meeting our monthly targets, more evidence that we are not good enough, not worthy and more falling short of the results that we want to achieve.

What we need to understand is that money is a reward for effort, not a goal. Not in the "you need to work hard for money" kind of way . When we live from our authentic self, the self that does not concern itself with fitting in, pleasing people, or how we look to the world, we learn to serve from a really genuine place. When we serve from this place, it is from our hearts, not from our ego. Serving from the heart will always reward us in many ways. One way is through always feeling grateful, balanced, and going through life from a place of love and understanding. The other way life rewards us is through bringing to us like-minded people, experience, adventure, and of course, money is just part of that. Money is NEVER the goal, but always the by-product of you being you.

Many times, people encourage the 'think positive, change your world' mantra. Unfortunately, life does not work by thinking alone. We must feel this on all levels of our being to make it part of our reality. One thing we do know from the way energy works is that our feelings carry much more energy value than just thoughts alone. We need both thoughts and feelings to bring about the positive change that we want in our lives.

Many of us try to think positively but deep down, we have contradicting beliefs. It is like looking in the mirror and telling yourself that you love the body you see, but in your head, you know that you want your arms to be toner, your thighs to be smaller, and your waistline to be thinner. Beware: While you can fake it until you make it with those around you, you cannot convince yourself out of something that you innately feel and believe. Being truthful with yourself is imperative. It is not about being hard on yourself but being consciously aware of the ways that you think and feel. This level of honestly with yourself gives you so much power to change your inner world and therefore your outer experience.

There are so many reasons why we think, feel and act the way we do. Society and environment of our upbringing are major contriutors to our thought and belief processes. This does not mean we need to surrender to what society has deposited in us—no. Instead, we have the ability take responsibility for ourselves and increase our conscious awareness around ourselves and others around us. This will not only help us understand how we were constructed but also give us the awareness to modify, change and reconstruct our internal world. The truth is we have been groomed and conditioned into the person that we are today. We also have beliefs, values, programs, mannerisms, actions, and feelings that make up who we are. What we have never been taught is to question any of these consciously, rather than automatically consume them, whether they are beneficial to us or not.

However, our culture, religion, and nationality play key roles in our lives; it is not all bad. Even if you are going through despair right now, there is something in your life to be grateful for. Even reading this book can help you alter your path forward and change the trajectory of your life. Even if you have been through the depths of despair, ask yourself how this experience is benefitting you right now and take note of the synchronicities along the way, guiding you through this moment in time.

The question is: 'Is the person that got you here, the same person you want to get you through the next six to twelve months of your life and beyond? This is your choice to make. Every single one of us can change any belief, any value, any thought pattern that seems to be getting in the way of our path forward. Let us face it. These thoughts are blocking you from achieving everything you deserve to experience in this life.

In part two of this book, you can have a look at where the discomforts live within your mind and physical body when your soul is calling you to reconnect. This will help you understand yourself a little bit more.

On some level, we already know what is going on within us, sometimes we need this to rise to the surface as a reminder and then we can work through it. I do believe that most of the time what you read on your discomforts may not be all new information, but more confirmation for you.

Support

From the time of our birth, we have learnt to lean on the people around us. We need to learn how to eat, what to eat, we learn to fall asleep, to dress ourselves, to read and write. We learn to navigate through this physical world. However, sometimes there comes a point where support and guidance can start to seem more like control, guiding us a little bit too far in the direction that others want rather than teaching us to connect to our intuition and trust ourselves and our own inner direction.

Many of us never learnt the difference between guidance on our path and what is good for us, which is guidance from within, and closing a skills gap which we can seek assistance from others.

In business this shows up a lot in marketing. Marketing strategies are a skills gap, what marketing strategy is right for you and your business at its current stage is an inner guidance.

A time will come when you need to learn to trust and support yourself again. A lot of us miss out on this lesson in our younger years. This is a lesson that most of us miss out on in our younger years. We go from our parents to marrying a partner that supports us in a very similar way to what our parents did. Our 20s are meant to be a time of deep personal discovery and growth. Durng this time, we learn to understand who we are, what our roles within the community are and how to help the world around us. We are all different in our journeys but very similar on the inside. These different journeys are what make us special and unique, we've been taught on some level that we must fit in, be normal, be the same as everyone else. This has disconnected you from who you are, and we end up playing a role that we feel we are 'supposed to.'

We put so much pressure on ourselves to fit in during the most important growth years of our life. Instead of growing into confident, self-trusting beings, we struggle to find our place, seeking guidance and validation from our parents, partners, friends, colleagues, and society. We learn that a partner completes us, as in the case of two halves coming together to make a whole, romantising the fact that we are broken and incomplete just as we are. A lot of my clients in their 40s they regain their confidence as they spent their a lot of their 30s understanding and relearning that they are perfect just the way they are and no longer need input from others to know what they really want in life. They learn that it comes from within.

The time has come for you to learn that you are 100% whole, that you are not broken. You are complete and perfect just the way you are, you do not have to play any role. You do not have to play the role of the leader, the introvert, the extrovert, the life of the party, the mother, the business owner etc. All these roles are not who we really are. You are perfect just being you—without the label, without the clothes, without status, without the fancy car, without the big house—none of this has got anything to do with who you are at your core. It is time to strip down those layers and reconnect with your true self. Your intuition will guide you to where you need to go. If you need extra knowledge, your intuition will guide you there, and once you get there, it will feel perfectly right for you.

One time, I spoke to my business coach about social media marketing. I told him social media content ideas and topics that I was unsure whether to create or not. The introvert side of me thought that being too blunt may seem offensive, but my leader's side thought it would be great content that people need to hear. When we identified that I was executing my business ideas from these two standpoints—the introvert and the leader—it was much easier to identify which role I took up at different times. This brought me a much broader conscious awareness of how I was doing things, and if something was not working out in my business, I would simply ask myself which role I was playing at the time. By identifying where I was, I could return to my centre and re-execute from a place of authenticity, which is the part of me that does not play a role at all.

This was one uplevelled I had, business became easier because there was so much less resistance. All the tasks that I needed to do just flowed with ease as it was now coming from a real place, and not from a place that was put on.

This is what I intend for you. I want you to discover that you can fully support yourself. Imagine a business that is flowing with ease no matter how much work is required because you are no longer adding in extra energy of playing a role.

THE WORLD EXISTS AS YOU PERCEIVE IT.
IT IS NOT WHAT YOU SEE...
BUT HOW YOU SEE IT.
IT IS NOT WHAT YOU HEAR...
BUT HOW YOU HEAR IT.
IT IS NOT WHAT YOU FEEL...
BUT HOW YOU FEEL IT.

—RUMI

LIFE PATH

We all want to live a fulfilled, balanced life. Many people envision a balanced life as spending enough time with our family, at work, with our friends—basically spending time how we wish rather than spending all our hours executing our business. When we learn to support ourselves, we understand that it is not about time but more about energy dissipation and flow.

The biggest problem today is that we fill our time with low priority tasks and tasks that are not aligned to who we are, not aligned to our dreams, values, desires, or life path. They are aligned with what we have learnt that we should have and not what we want. We have been conditioned to please people without realising it. Therefore, we end up living their lives, dreams, ambitions, and beliefs. It takes conscious questioning and self-inquiry to bring this internal paradigm to a halt and redirect it back on a path that is purely aligned to you.

You are here for a purpose, as an individual and a greater part of the collective. To live this life with the conscious awareness that is going to propel you through every stage because when you move forward from a creative mindset, you are less likely to live from the back seat, from a reactive standpoint where you feel that you are continually putting out fires and fixing things rather than creating what you would like to experience. A creative mindset puts you in a state of flow and abundance, which others would call 'lucky'. However, you are creating your own luck. The word 'create' means to cause something to come into being or not made by an ordinary process. To have an extraordinary life, you need to create it; it will not happen automatically.

Here, you will explore your life path and how to live from a creative standpoint. This does not mean that you have to figure out your entire life from where you stand right now as that can be very daunting. Living your life intentionally in segments, think the next hour, tomorrow, next two months, or next six months.

I started my career as a fashion designer because I loved seeing the end product on people. I particularly loved seeing how they felt when they wore the clothes I designed. I remember walking into a shopping mall and seeing a little girl wearing a purple skirt that I designed that season. The way she twirled in that skirt brought joy to my heart. Just knowing I could impact one life like that made me feel so good inside.

I feel my journey today is no different. I am simply utilising a different skill set. I still help people find joy in their lives. I do not look back at my 15 years of designing and see it as a waste of time. I see a stepping-stone to where I am now. I left the industry because I lost the joy. My time felt more consumed with finances and budget than creating a masterpiece for those little girls to twirl in. This is why it is important for me to follow that feeling, to move away from the feeling of disconnect in my work into that feeling of joy again, and that feeling led me right here. My intension is to help people find their joy and to feel it myself along the way.

Your Path

What is your life purpose? What is it that you wish to achieve? Who do you want to 'be' while achieving it? It is essential to ask yourself why you started this business in the first place! What is the highest purpose of your business and life? What do you really want to get out of it?

When you strip back the layers and roles, you can answer these questions authentically and really feel into what is in alignment for you. There are many ups and downs to life and business, so you need to understand your 'why.' When you have a compelling 'why', you can withstand almost any 'how'. If there is one thing I have learnt in business, it is to enjoy the rockiness of the path. Enjoying the growth and learning the reasons behind the failures and mistakes. We know they are not really failures if we learn from it. They are opporutinties to expand.

Knowing and connecting to your purpose will help you feel your way through life. When asking yourself one simple question - How do I feel right now? Are you feeling the way you want to feel? If you are feeling the way you want to feel and are where you want to be then you are on the right path. If not, it may be time to re-evaluate what you are doing or your perspective. Some situations in life are perfectly imperfect. Some events may not feel good but present life lessons and an opportunity to expand beyond your current confort zone.

When we gain that level of clarity on our future, it enables us to create a path forward. With this it allows us to create boundaries that keep us on track. It give clarity to what you want in your life and what you do not want. This can be projected into any are of life, from food, people, places, values, beliefs, work environments, everything. When we have this level of clarity it gives us more trust within ourselves on the decisions we make not only on a big scales but also the everyday decisions as well.

Clairty = Boundaries = Self Trust

Your purpose is usually much greater than you. You may not be able to fulfil it in this lifetime, but knowing that you are living on purpose gives you ultimate direction and enables you to live your authentic, confident life.

Lifestyle

When you look at serving the world through your business, you need to evaluate your entire life to ensure it is all in balance. What is balance? Balance is anything you want it to be. Ther eis no formular but they formular you want to give it.

How do you want your business to work in with the rest of your life? What else do you have to consider—spouse, kids, hobbies, friends, health, fitness, socialising etc? This balanced perspective of business needs to be formed as early as possible. If your lifestyle is not balanced, your mental and physical balance will be impaired, as well as the soundness of your mind. While everyone's perception of balance is different, it is important to determine what works for you.

Most of us want to reach a benchmark of achievement before brining in that balance. If I work hard for the next three to six months to get the business up and going, then I will cut back the hours. 'I'll wait until we reach x,y,z before taking a break', 'I'll wait until we make the next deal and then I will focus on myself', 'I'll do it after the busy season', 'Let me get through the quiet season then...' Before you know it, business is turning in two million dollars in revenue, and you are so stressed out, time-poor, and feel so isolated from everyone you care about.

From the outset, you need to know what balance means to you and how your business fits into this balance of your life. Here is a tip: It is not about how you spend your time, but how do you spend your energy.

By changing the perspective of how we see what we do, we release the pressure we put on ourselves and allow a freer flow. Many of us are consumed by the word 'business' because we feel it means that we need to perform—need to achieve a certain budget or accolade. While this is nice, what we need to look at first is how to serve.

Balance

We spoke a lot about obtaining balance within Lifestyle, to learn to work out how you want your life to be and balance things according to your inner desires. I will reiterate here that it is not about how much time that we feel we have or do not have but about how you spend your energy. Where your attention goes, your energy flows. This gives an idea of what consumes you the most and the required adjustments to obtain the balance that you desire. We are creatures of balance and contrast. We need this external balance to help maintain the internal balance and therefore help our physical, emotional, mental, and spiritual bodies to not just survive but to thrive. It is just like food. We cannot just eat apples all day every day; we need a balance of nutrients to provide the body with what it needs to function optimally. We know when we have overindulged on food because our bodies tell us so. Our life is no different. When we focus on one area too much and neglect other areas, our emotions and body will let us know.

To thrive and obtain that internal/external balance, we need to connect with ourselves deeper than the emotional level. When we know what we want out of life, it is so much easier to say 'Yes' to the things that energetically align with that path and to say 'No' to the things that do not. When we do this, we work from a more meaningful place. We come from the understanding that we know why we do what we do, why we connect with the people that we do.

We tend to feel out of balance when we have people, things, thoughts, and feelings in our world that we do not want, need or energetically block our flow. When we keep things that we do not want, we become unbalanced and things do not go the way we want them to. It is time to stop 'putting-up' with things that do not feel right. Toss them out, look at things differently, transcend the feeling, or heal the wounds and unblock your path. While there are times were we may need to feel it to heal it, it is not worth sitting in a place of discomfort for longer than needed. The sooner we can complete the emotional cycles and realign to our path the more life will flow in your direction.

Back in my days of designing, there was a time I felt so isolated, and to be honest with you, I was a grumpy little bitch. The by-product of that was constant arguments with my partner. I had so much anger and resentment in my system that my stomach function was breaking down. It was not until years later that I realised I had fructose malabsorption.

My external world was reflecting my inner world. I was so disconnected from self at the time. The only way life gets our attention if we miss our intuitive signs and keep ignoring emotional signs is by manifesting in the physical—that was a severly inflammed gut for me. The more I learnt to heal the core emotions and the events around them the more my life began to flow more effortlessly. It is so much easier to move forward when we are not carrying decades of baggage with us.

Passion

What are you hungry for? What do you want to achieve? What do you want to change in the world? How do you want to help people? What the people problems you can solve? What do people come to you for?

I find it interesting that there are always two answers whenever I ask these questions. The first answer is what they see on the surface; the house, car, financial independence, happy family, the freedom etc. This stems from beliefs and values that no longer serve them. The second answer comes from the heart, a part of us that does not sleep—the part that keeps knocking, but is often ignored. The part of us that really wants to make a difference.

Your passion underlies your life path. It is your driving force. Your passion is your 'why'. Why are you doing your business? Why are you living where you are? Why do you surround yourself with the people around you? Your passion underpins your whole life's existence. It helps you make decisions on what you do, eat, drink, who you relate with and who you do not. It drives you to be the person you want to be, the person you need to be to fulfill your life's path. It ignites the spark within you to enable you play big and not keep your knowledge and talents to yourself.

You are here to share your knowledge and talents, to be of service to those around you. Your passion will provide you with the most trust and confidence to act towards your dreams.

I love you. Yes, self-love is one part of passion, but the passion we refer to here goes far beyond self-love and the love that we share with others. It is the deep connection to your life path that it becomes your primary focus. Your passion stems from being in alignment with your life's purpose. It stems from truly knowing yourself; mind, body, spirit, and energies. It is the true understanding of who you are, where you come from, and where you are going.

Trust complements passion. Trust that everything and everyone in your path is your teacher and is guiding you to your ultimate adventure. It is the unlearning and relearning of how to live from our soul and higher self, to have abundant human experiences—our own personal truth.

My passion became clearer after I left designing with health problems. After my diagnosis and being told that I need to change my diet, something did not sit right with me. Knowing that I had to be on a restricted diet for the rest of my life did not make sense. At this stage, I knew very little about health. Hence, this was the first time in my life I started to question things. My thought was, if I was not born this way, I should not have to stay this way. I felt like it was my duty to uncover the truth—the truth of why I was suffering and how I could heal. I felt like I was on the wrong path. I started cutting through the noise of society. One thing I have learnt is that the physical body is much smarter than it is credited for. When we give it a balanced environment, it thrives.

We are spiritual beings having a human experience and our souls inhabit our physical bodies. This helps us to realise that nothing is permanent. When we have completed this experience, we no longer need our body and therefore will return back to source.

The love we have for the fullness of who we are and our passion comes from knowing that we can create a magnificent adventure out of this life and this body.

Study and Knowledge

Study and knowledge constitute two main areas: the knowledge you obtain via external sources (schools, courses, formal education, the knowledge and wisdom from others around you) and the internal growth from your experiences (self-actualisation).

The external sources around study and knowledge is about learning new skills and obtaining resournces. It is about accumulating tools to help us along our journey.

When we look at marketing, obtaining knowledge and skills about how to market our business is not about doing things one way or another, but rather about building a library of reasuoruces that we can intuitively pull from.

However, over time we have learnt that all the answers to lifes questions is something that we seek externally. That others hold more wisdom and answers about us then we do.

Other people help us close our skills gaps; ways to market, how to tie our shoe laces, how to built a house, ways to obtain inner clarity. Ultimately, you need to learn to connect in, use all the infromation learnt and then understand on how this applies or does not apply to you right now.

Alternatively, there are many times in clinic where I have seen clients confuse a state of stress for a lack in skills. This especially shows up around communication and not feeling heard, when what we need at time is to learn to communicate more effecty.

Then there is athe knowledge we obtain through the journey of life itself. I have been introduced to people who leave me with a little piece of wisdom shortly after our first encounter. I have also spent a years with some other people, learning from and developing with them. Both connections can have similar levels of impact. Learning is not a factor of time, but experience and awareness.

Nothing happens by accident. Every occurrence is an opportunity to learn and grow. Even the most treacherous of times can give you the strength and courage to soar higher. When you can look at life from this perspective, it is much easier to move forward from fear, pain, and turmoil. You can step into your greatness. Yes, YOU.

In the modern world, we have become accustomed to using study and knowledge as a baseline before we know who we are in the world. Statistics show that 75% of people are stuck in jobs, with the mindset that a job should not necessarily be what you love to do but something that you have to do to make ends meet. When we start to learn who we are and what we stand for, it is so much easier to expand our mind and our awareness by acquiring more knowledge and study that supports our beliefs and mission. This is where the real difference is made. This is where we learn to live fulfilled lives with flow.

SOME ENTREPRENEURS THINK,
HOW CAN I MAKE A LOT OF MONEY?
BUT THE BETTER WAY IS TO THINK IS,
HOW CAN I MAKE PEOPLE'S LIVES
A LOT BETTER?
IF YOU GET IT RIGHT,
THE MONEY WILL COME.

—RICHARD BRANSON

BUSINESS

Here, the essence of business will be explored. How does business play a role in our lives and how does our business help us travel on our life path?

What is business? I do not know about you, but for me, I was told by society that business was this great thing where you create a product or service, hustle your arse off to sell it, reap the rewards, and retire early in life with the lifestyle that you have always craved.

But, what is business, really?

I see passion and purpose as the feminine and business as the masculine. When we learn to understand who we are are, we a start to connect in with that passion and purpose, we know what impact we want to have in the world and how we want to live, we then can execute that passion and purpose, which is the role of our businesses. When we know what difference we want to make, business becomes the driving tool to achieve that difference. Business facilitates a wider reach and helps you connect with more people. Without business, we cannot bring our gifts into the world and make the impact we desire that we personally want to make.

Business strips us bare, just like relationships. It uncovers so many wounds and beliefs that we hold about ourselves and the world, that work for us and ones that do not. If we do not do the inner work, we will always struggle to meet our goals and be pushed into hustle mode. Every deal we make and every client we onboard will consume so much time and energy that we will end up drained, overwhelmed, fatigued and resentful.

We have been taught not only to hustle in business, but we have also been taught that marketing will make or break our business. This goes alongside ensuring that you have the right business systems, are consistent with showing up on social media etc. I want to challenge your belief here. The 'work' that needed to be done it that of aligning your beliefs that are blocking the flow of your business. When you are aligned to your business andgoals, you become magnetic, visabile and connect with people that easily covert into clients and customers.

Over the years, the more I have done the inner work, the more my business has scaled with less effort. When there is no resistance between where you are and the goals that you wish to achieve, it manifests in your life effortlessly. The ideas just flow in, the opportunities present themselves, the amazing clients are attracted to you and the deals come together with effortless ease and flow.

I was told for many years that I was too much of an introvert to be successful in business and that I should just give up. For a long time, I believed that and worked even harder just to get some sort of mediocre results. One day, I found myself in reflection and I realised that I was never an introvert. I am a highly sensitive extrovert hanging around the wrong people. When I am with the right people, I am in my element. I can talk for days and am energised. On the other hand, when I am with people that do not align with I am quite shy, quiet, and I get drained really quickly. Once I realised this, my whole perception of myself changed, my clientele changed, started to attract clients that I absolutely adore and many of them have become friends, business became fun again and I got better boundaries around who I connect with, to ensure I spend time with aligned people.

Now, this had nothing to do with changing my avatar, changing the way I marketed, or who I was marketing to—but I changed. I changed the way I saw me and that energy shift changed my business.

I believe when working on your business, 70% efforts needs to be on personal development and 30% on strategy and you will noticed the lap it takes.

Most entrepreneurs in the early phase get stuck in fear and find it very difficult to move forward from this place. Fear of not knowing how to market, fear of not knowing the business basics, fear of putting themselves out there, fear of failure, fear of success, fear of making money from their natural gifts and talents and feeling that they 'should' know it all. They find it hard to ask for help. The interesting thing here is that these fears and limiting beliefs do not affect just startups. They can cripple any business at any stage and every level. The scenario just looks slightly different, with more at stake, more money, more people and more responsibility.

A lot of startups know that they want to serve and help people but do not know how to run or build a business. They get stuck in practitioner mode serving their clients and fear the transition over to business mode to build and grow the business. They build a job for themselves rather than a business that serves. They find this intimidating, and it hinders their progress. This is where we need to assess what is best for us. Do you need to have a business to serve the world or are you better off contributing your zone of genius to a company that is aligned to your values? This is where we need to be honest with ourselves and reassess, remembering there is no right or wrong answer; rather, there are only answers that is right for you right now.

However, if lack of strategy or knowledge in this area is the only thing holding you back, it is important to remember that by doing the inner work, by being in alignment with your business, you will attract the resources required for you to thrive and grow. The alignment of your business will draw to you resources both external and internally to assist you in creating the right strategy for you and to help you learn and thrive in this space.

Last year, I needed an influencer to help me grow my business. I asked around and searched tirelessly for the right person. The more inner work I did around self-worth, communication and interaction with people, the more my stars aligned. That was when she fell into my world. The conversation was effortless. I did not feel needy. Everything seemed just right. Doing the inner work makes it easier for growth to occur in your business. You will still need to do the work, to execute the strategies, but you will learn to have fun doing so. You will learn to ask the right questions when you encounter a roadblock. Instead of 'what do I need to do here?', you will ask, 'What part of me is out of alignment here?' 'What thought, belief or pattern needs to shift?'

It is important to realise that it takes much more than a great business strategy and market conditions to make the impact you want. It is also crucial to make sure the ensure that the machine is well oiled and functioning at optimal level. The machine that I am referring to is you. When you know you have a duty to make an impact in the world, we need to have a look at who we need to be and how we need to look after ourselves to be able to create that impact.

We are not superhuman, but human beings wanting to serve the world and create an amazing place for ourselves at the same time. However, as a business owner, you become your number one priority. Everything lands on you. If you sink so does your life and your business. It is important to listen to yourself and look after your mind, body and soul to maintain stability and balance.

As you grow and strengthen, so does your business. There is no separation between you and your business. Your business can push you to imbalance or it can push you to become the best person you can be. When the result of doing the inner work manifests in your personal life and business, you will notice it was worth taking the time to create everything just the way you want it to be. It is such a good feeling to be able to bake your cake with love, and then you get to sit and enjoy eating it too.

When you do the inner work, you will see the improvements in how you connect with prospective clients. 'Sales conversations' will no longer seem like hard work but an enjoyable connective conversations with great people that you get to help. Your reach will improve, your sales results will skyrocket, and the impact of your work will grow. You end up building a life that you do not need a holiday from, but because it brings you joy and freedom.

Your Ideal Client

Our aim in business is to work with our 'ideal' client, the one that we cannot wait to see again, the one that energises us and makes business a pleasure. However, that does not happen all the time. While some customers are great, there are some clients that do not align with us. The irony of this is that they are still aligned to us in some way. Our customers are our mirrors. They reflect our wounds, our strength, our alignments and misalignments. They will always show us where we need to do the inner work to not only grow within ourselves and our business, but to also experience growth and help others on their journey.

One part specifically that this can bring up for us is our inner boundaries. Many entrepreneurs welcome just anyone as customer to make profit, but this is not a long-term growth strategy. By doing this, we end up resenting our clients and business, becoming stressed, overwhelmed, and in turn, delivering substandard products and services. We want to serve clients that we love—clients whom we earnestly wish to succeed. By tightening our boundaries and saying no to clients that are not aligned, we establish precise intentions on who we wish to work with. We can serve from a place of clarity and vision. We are also letting the universe know what exactly we want and in turn, we will continue to attract more aligned clients.

You probably know your customer demographics. Here, you need to ask yourself a different question: 'What energy does my customer bring?' If they walking into a room, how would I notice them? What are their beliefs and values? What is their intention? Are you aligned to that customer?

I have had many clients that would like to work with, high ticket customers but believed I was not good enough to work with these kind of customers. Some struggle to work with people that earn more than them, have a higher status or even look better than them. These can be fundament blocks to receiving valued clients into your business. Once you work through these, and understand that they are no different to you and I, the gates open to allow an inflow of new amazing customers. Now, this has nothing to do with our actual marketing or business strategy, but everything to do with our energy and therefore what we are attracting to or repelling from our business. It will as a by product create certainty and a higher quality of languaging in your marketing copy.

If you attract unideal clients, they will not only drain your energy and time, but also take up your dairy space and leave no room or energy for your IDEAL customer to flow in. The unideal consumers change the energy of your business, brand and, ultimately, you.

You can start by creating a list of your customers, putting the best at the top and your least favourite at the bottom. The best ones are the ones that you love working with and that spend the most money with you. They are your biggest advocates. The ones you get excited when you see them in your calender. You can then have a look at removing the ones at the bottom of the list. The ones that take up a lot of time, sometimes more then needed and the spend is very little. I find the best way to do this is to refer them to someone who may be a better match. When you do this, you will not only feel lighter, and you will create openings both energetically and time-wise for new, more ideal consumers to flow in.

Doing this may create a feeling of nervousness, especially if you rely on your income. You may feel like you are pushing away your potential customers. Nonetheless, you must develop trust in yourself. Trust comes easier when we have a clear vision of what we want and where we want to go as well as boundaries that keep us on track.

When you know who your ideal customer is and what they energetically feel like, it is much easier to say 'no' to people that are not them. By saying 'no' to one person you are letting the universe know that you are saying 'yes' to those that are a better match for you and your business.

There are multiple ways to let go of 'bottom list' customers. You can let them go all at once, or you can simply do one at a time. It is all about what feels right for you.

A couple of years ago, I had a percular client. I could tell her heart was not in the sessions, and I felt she was coming for the wrong reasons. Our values were not aligned and even though I knew this at the beginning, I gave her the benefit of the doubt to see where we could take this and hopefully bring her forward along her journey. A week before her second session, I wrote a friendly email to her checking in on her, seeing how she was doing after her initial session and giving her the option to continue or cancel her next session. I trusted this was going to give both of us the outcome we needed—an out for her and an out from my diary. Within ten minutes of receiving her email to cancel her session, two new clients booked in. They matched my idea of an 'ideal client'.

The lesson here for me as that holding on to one client that was not in alignment was actually taking up the energetic space of two or more ideal clients. I learnt to release attachment to the perciveved outcome and trust that the right outcome will present itself. I wanted to work with more people, but needed to trust that by letting go of one that wasn't right, actually meant more would come my way. Our job is to be true to ourselves, to remain in alignment. Outcomes are a by-product of alignment and flow, to take actions that are in alignment with us to keep the flow and the outcome is an easily reached by-product of that alignment and flow.

Fees

Fees are a subset of strategy. This is an area of business that we both overthink and under strategies. Sometimes, we make our prices so much about us and tend to forget that we are actually running a business that has overheads, requires profit for growth and expansion and that you also need to take an income from it.

There are five main sections here:

1. Lifestyle
2. Self-worth
3. Customer
4. Who you want to serve
5. Profit

Lifestyle

I spoke about lifestyle earlier. You need to evaluate the cost of your lifestyle and how much time you invest in your business. From here, you can determine how much to charge for your products and services. There is no point charging a low rate for one on one clients if you can only do 20 a week and want a high-end lifestyle.

In this part, we can step into our masculine strategy energy to work out the foundations. It is important to determine how the feminine energy feels within you. What emotions are spurred in you as you work out your prices from a strategic perspective?

Self-worth

The feminine side of us is about the receiving moeny, which you will start feeling into the triggers around pricing as you strategize it. It is important to notice what is coming up for you?

In today's age, money is very much tied to our self-worth. It is very important for you to do the inner work to facilitate abundant flow of your business. Many of us block our flow because we select pricing, services and clients based on how we perceive ourselves. If you are pushing yourself down, if you are feeling like an imposter, if you are feeling too greedy or have a fear of success (many people fear success than failure), then your business will not flow. The more you work on improving your self-worth, the more your business flows.

Remember business is not about us, it's about the customer. When we remove ourselves and how we perceive ourselves from the equation we can easily connect in the prices that work for both us and our customers. We can sell the same service at $5 or $5000 there is a market for both. As we grow and evolve so does our prices and our customer.

Your Customer

The problem that you are solving for your customer, how much is that worth to them?

One of my clients requested that I organize a launch package. The package was aimed at aligning to her goals, as well as releasing blocks and unwanted beliefs during the launch week. For those who have launched products or services, you will understand how much of an emotional roller-coaster the week can be. I devised an outline of the support package and asked how much she was willing to pay for it. She offered a price which was double my current rate. Sometimes, we underestimate the value we give to our clients and what it means to them to have their problem solved. Do not guess, ask!

Who do you want to Serve?

Here is a scenario: What if you've done all the above, but you are still not loving the kind of clients you attract? What do you do?

Back in the client section, we discussed our ideal client. There, we understand that the price is meaningful for us AND the client.

When I started out, my rates were low. I was comfortable with that because I was new to the industry and still figuring things out. My clients never had an issue with my pricing (probably because it was too low), but I did get a lot of reschedules and I did not love some of the clients. I thought they perceived my service as a last resort and were not really dedicated to the process of health and development—like a magic pill theraphy. I wanted more growth-focused clients. I found that along the years when as I raised my prices, the quality of clients I attracted also improved.

Along the line, I had to work on my self-worth to interact with the higher quality clients. At the beginning, it made me nervous. They had strong motives, were inspiring, knew exactly what they wanted and expected results. While I was result-driven, my previous clients were not as focused and determined as the new clients I attracted. But I absoluelty loved them, because we worked, they listened and results came fast.

Sometimes, the universe nudges you to step up, to upgrade the way you see yourself. You need to ask yourself the important question: 'Who would I love to work with and who do I need to become to work with these people?'

Profit

Just how much profit do you need? How much profit do you want? How much do you want to grow? How many people do you want to serve?

These are questions to ask yourself when setting your prices. You did not come into this business to serve one or two clients. You came here to make a difference. What does that difference look like? If you are reading this book, this is your cue to step up and lead!

Close your eyes. When you see yourself in your mind's eye leading your community, what does that look like? How many people are there? What you see will be just one level of your growth and your businesses growth.

Growth does cost, this is for you to work out what is the price of growth is and factor that in.

Products and Services

What problem are you helping people solve? How are you going to solve their problem? Are you helping people be pain free, lift their confidence, heal from emotional eating? The more clarity you gain here, the easier it is for you to innovate products and offer services that actually solve probems.

There are two major determinants. They are:

1. What problem they think needs to be solved

2. What problem they actually need solving from a practitioners perspective

Our problem-solving strategies as business owners have to align with what is best for our clients. There is the way we as a business owners and practitioners want to solve someones problem and then there is what is the best way for them? How are they going to get the most of out of this? What experience to we need to give them for them to create the shift and transformation within themselves.?

You must understand the difference between what your clients want and what they actually need to solve their problem. While someone with back pain may want to simply take a magic pill, they need to work on trapped emotions to obtain a more permant result. How do you deliver that effective permanent result for your client?

The third factor is how you want to solve their problem. This often comes in when we look at how we want to consult. There are many consultants out there that do not like one on one session and prefer the freedom that group work provides and they know they can get good results in that environment. While others see the power in a personalised service and love to have their week filled up with clients appointments.

I had one therapist that saw 40 one-hour clients per week and she loved it. She thrived off that sort of workload. I have another client that hosts multiple online courses and shows up to hundreds of people at once for one hour per week and that is her ultimate work zone.

There is no right or wrong, just what works for you and your clientel. Personally, I love the depth I get from working one-on-one with a therapist. I never opt in to group programs. There was a time I enrolled in a group theraphy, but I dropped out and switched to a personalized session. Your clients are a reflections of you, so understanding your preference is normally the same preference for your clients. Why would you offer a group program if you don't like joining one yourself?

Developing our products and services can induce many triggers. We will discuss this in more detail. Crises that arise when we try to develop our products and services include:

Am I good enough?

Do I have enough qualifications?

If I do just one more course, I will attract more people!

What if no one what's to buy the course or session?

Our beliefs around the product and the product value goes hand in hand. I know people (who had many great product ideas but did not think anyone would need it or pay for it even before doing the market research. We let our doubts make our decisions for us instead of the people. We let shame, embarrassment and fear of failure hold us to ransom and we end up in a state of paralysis. We know that what we have to offer works but are so scared of what others' opinions and thoughts may be.

When we shift the focus from us and how we will win, fail or feel to the customer, things start to get easier. What do they need? How do they need it? What are their goals? What do they need from you today?

In life, you show up for you. In business, you show up for them. Business is your service to the world. The moment you make it about you, is the moment you fail. As David R. Hawkins mentions in Success Is for You, success is not something you strive for, it is something you embody in the here and now. It is the attitude, energy and the way we go through life and business.

We struggle because we have underlying fears. In part two of this book, I will explain more of the emotions that arise from putting out your products and services and dealing with an ideal customer. In a nutshell, this phase of life results in questioning of self-worth and diminished enthusiasm from looking to the past too often, which leads to repetition of past mistakes. Emotions like regret, guilt and depression govern this area of our business and hold us back if left unhealed.

Many years ago, I was so focused on the results of my business rather than the results my clients needed. I tried to maximize my time by offering my service to a lot of people in the limited time I had. I found myself creating mediocre courses and masterminds to fill this void.

However, my business started to take off when I realised what my consumers needed, and that was healing and transformation. I understood that the personalized experiences I created were so powerful that anything else would not succeed. The more focus I put on my one on one work, the more my business grew. Still, I was stuck with serving many people at once, knowing fully well that it will not yield the best results.

To move forward, I had to increase my self-worth. I recognised the role I played in my life and let go of them—the mother, the wife, the healer, the leader, the introvert. I started to recognise when I was playing one of these roles and stepped back into my heart instead. This enabled me let go and step into my authentic self. I allowed myself just to be me.

I worked on healing the inner child that was told that her success meant other people's failure. I worked on many other beliefs around my self worth. For two days, I let all these beliefs precipitate out of my subconscious; I ended up with one and a half pages of these beliefs, sifting through them individually with the aim of dismantling them.

When we work from this healed place, we facilitate more alignment with our purpose and passion. We become more aligned with our clients and understand how they need to be served. I would come out of sessions with sparks of ideas on how to serve them better, not only in our sessions but also in a group environment. I understood that for the people that I was serving, some of them needed to hear what other people were going through. This would help them heal, grow and understand that other people have the same problem—that they are not alone. This would encourage them to grow, heal and move forward.

As I mentioned above, one of the reasons we dwell in this fear is because we focus on the past and grow fearful of moving forward. We fear because we are too focused on ourselves. All my clients have this block in some part of their business journey. What happens if they judge me? What if I cannot solve the problem? What if they think I am wrong? Am I good enough? Will they get enough out of our sessions? Will they be able to afford it? These are a few of the questions that hold us back. Instead, why not ask yourself how your clients want to be served. What do I need to know right now? How do they want the service to be delivered?

When we turn the focus table around, we learn to understand that business is not about us; it is about how we can serve the clients in the best possible way. When the focus is 100% on the customer and their needs, the fear dissipates. There is no fear of failure, fear of being wrong, fear of not being enough, fear of putting ourselves other there. Fear gives way for service.

Every individual has an energy system that attracts and repels people, objects and experiences. It is important to understand that as business owners, we are the face of the business. We attract and repel our clients to us and our work. When you operate from a place of fear, you attract fearful clients. So the question I ask you is, how do you feel about your products/services and the price/value you have placed on them?

Many of us seem confident on the surface, but deep down, we are riddled with self-doubt. Unfortunately, energy does not lie; you can only pretend for so long. But, you will always attract things, people and experiences that match your energy and beliefs, not your façade. When we start to work through the underlying issues and love ourselves for who and what we truly are, our outer world will reflect that.

Financial Goals

Earning money is one of the biggest stressors in business, resulting in mental, emotional and energy blocks. This includes the stress of providing for oneself, staff and family. The main instigator of this stress is misaligned focus; we lose sight of the purpose of our business and become hell-bent on making the good money. The main reason for this is we take our focus off the reason we are in business in the first place become solely focused and even obsessed with attracting money. This will be discussed in more detail in the next chapter. However, it is important to remember that money is a by-product of business and a reward for problem solving.

Money can be used as a tool. Marketing and communication facilitate communication with potential clients. Products bring clarity about how a client's problem can be solved. Our fees ensure we have the right energy exchange, while financial goals allow us to grow our business. The main purpose of growing our business is to reach more people, to help more people and to create a bigger impact in lives. This is the lives of our clients, our staff, our families and ours as well.

Thoughts of expansion through financial goals are often accompanied by a feeling of regret. We do not feel worthy enough to embark on our goals. We are so good at holding ourselves back and not backing ourselves 100%. We listen to the voice in our head, which is not even ours. For so long, we have been taught to please others, to dress for others, to present ourselves in a manner that is acceptable to others, hence, we forget who we are.

Self-doubt is actually not our voice but the accumulated voices of others that sit inside us for so long and rear its ugly head at every opportuinity. That primary school teacher that told you to never draw again because you had no talent, or your mum that gave you a dismissive 'that's great' when you tried to show her how fast you could run. All these little incidences can hold us back from doing relatively simple things as we grow older.

When we learn to focus on the relationship between ourselves and our source, we not only expand our awareness of ourselves but with this expansion, we learn to hold more space for more energy to flow to us. In business, this means more clients, more refined products and services and more growth.

We unlearn all those voices in our head and relearn that we are limitless. That we have this innate superpower to create the life we want and that our emotions are a guidance system always directing us on our forward path. They are showing you what thoughts are real and what thoughts are taking you away from your true self. Your true self does not have self-doubt nor does it tear you down. Your true self is encouraging, uplifting and motivating. Your true self is unconditional love.

A few years ago, I worked with a psychic reader who wanted to expand her business. There was one big block standing in her way: She had not told any of her family members that she was psychic in for fear of judgement. Therefore, she was conditionally marketing herself. Having the intension that every time she put out a piece of content to advertise her services that she didn't want her family to see it. Eventually, no one saw her business.

If we putting the intension out there that we don't want one person to see our work, we are actually telling the universe we don't want anyone to see our work.

After we spoke about coming out to her family, things totally shifted within her business. She opened up to her family, and to her greatest surprise, they were fine with it. Her confidence soared. She now having to turn down clients as her books were full. She was no longer sending mixed signals to the universe, and her content was seen by those who needed her guidance and support.

We are very good at making up people's mind for them. On what part of us they will accept and wont. When we learn to just be ourselves, we will attract those who resonate and repel those who are not a match. We do not need to actively do it; the universe has our back here. What we need to do is to be open and ready to accept what is here for us.

When you analyse your financial goals, you need to ask yourself, how many people do I want to help? How many can I energetically hold space for? Through this, you can quantify your financial goals to ensure that all your expenses and profits are clear. There is no progress without clarity. You can gain clarity by expanding your awareness and your capacity to hold space for others.

Marketing and Communications

When we first start up our business, we love our product, we are excited about how our product will work. We are excited to share it with the world, but how? The first few client may be easy to locate—then, we want more. Let us spread the word, have a bigger impact, build a bigger business, earn more money and create more freedom.

Some business owners spend a lot of time, energy and money on developing marketing strategies, and even allocate a fixed percentage of their earnings to marketing. They feel that marketing underpins business; the funnels, the lead generation, the sales calls, the advertising, the social media algorithms—but does it? If not handled with caution, this aspect of business can consume us and divert our focus from the impact we are really trying to have. We are consistently seeking ways to attract more customers, pass our message across and potray our brand message. We work so hard on this aspect, as we have been taught to believe that this is what expands our businesses.

What if business growth had nothing to do with this? What if business was about how open we are to receiving, rather than the method used to receive?

Let me ask you this...

How well do you receive a compliment? When someone says you look nice today, do you kindly receive the compliment or justify yourself? Do you easily allow someone to buy you a cup of coffee without feeling indebted to them? Can you do someone a favour without expecting anything in return? Do you say 'Yes' when you want to say 'No'? These are signs of people pleasing, which is us giving outwards because we have not been taught the art of receiving.

If we cannot simply receive just for being us, how can we easily receive the flow of clients that we desire? Yes, we can market to them, but if we do not learn to reiceve, either our marketing will not work or we will spend so much time, money and resources for very little result. The energetics behind the marketing message becomes pushy and desperate, even though they are technically perfect.

Marketing is about the energy behind the message and not the message itself. It is similar to that text message you receive, which you read five different times with different tones. Each time, the message feels different. What is your energy saying? Is it inviting people in or is it pushing people away?

I worked with a client who mentioned how she was envious of her competitor. Her competitor had this grand marketing plan, was all over social media and would outwardly express how she would easily make a million dollars on each program launch. However, when she investigated it further, she realised how much this competitor was spending on marketing compared to how much she was earning. She realised she had a bigger profit margin even so her takings was much less.

A million dollar launch is pointless if it outweighs your investment. It all comes down to our worth. Are you worth connecting with? Do you think you can solve the problem for your client? Are you good enough to do the job? Or do you always feel there is someone better? How we feel about ourselves will always reflect in who we attract into our lives.

I have seen so many clients try different marketing methods, write beautiful sales copies, post on social media consistently and get nothing. This is because when we do not value ourselves, our sabotage programs come into play. We hide ourselves; we post at strange times when very few people will see it. This is not a conscious thing, but a subconscious protection from our brain to keep us safe. If we do not value ourselves and put ourselves out there, we will feel unsafe, rejected and ridiculed. Your brain does not want this, so it will do everything it can with to keep you exactly where you are.

Understanding the 'how' of traditional marketing is a great tool to learn. It creates for us a bank of ideas to pull from when we are in alignment. The moment we start valuing ourselves, seeing our own self-worth and opening up to receive from other and the universe, the right 'how' will flow into your intuition. Intuition and knowledge are the perfect combination to create an amazing sales funnel and marketing campaign for yourself.

It starts with us and our alignment, then, the 'how'.

THE GREATEST REVOLUTION OF OUR
GENERATION IS THE DISCOVERY THAT
HUMAN BEINGS,
BY CHANGING THE INNER ATTITUDES
OF THEIR MINDS CAN CHANGE THE
OUTER ASPECTS OF THEIR LIVES.

—WILLIAM JAMES

FINANCES

Money is one of the top five stressors of the modern world. We have given money so much power and put so much pressure on ourselves to obtain it. We see how money and the value that we put on it affect the way we think, act, feel, the way we relate to one another and ultimately, the way we see ourselves compared to others.

We cannot focus on money as a sole entity without looking at our life path or how we will serve others. This is allowing our ego to rise and we end up building a business that is focused on self. Unfortunately, in the modern world, we have been nurtured into the survival of the fittest paradigm that helps us justify how we use the money to form a personal value system. We hold so many beliefs and values around money, what money means to us and how we should earn and deserve it. It has shifted our perspective from serving in alignment with our life path to 'How can I generate more money?'

The power that we have given money over our life is now determining how we think, feel and act. If we continue down this path, we end up chasing a life that will eventually feel out of alignment with who we are. We burn ourselves out , full of anxiety and disconnected from ourselves and the universe, alongside the many manifested physical side effects.

Money can be a beautiful tool to help us expand our reach, help others and provide the lifestyle we want for ourselves and our families. Money is a universal energy exchange for goods and services. In history, this energy exchange could be livestock, chocolate, gold, or rum. Now, it is paper with faces and numbers on it. It is purely a way of saying I give you this energy (livestock) for that energy (goods/services) because I value you and this exchange.

Business Goals

Firstly, it is essential to keep your feelings and personal interests out of your business goals and financial forecasts. We do this by addressing our underlying fears, concerns and doubts. This provides a clean slate and clear mind for goal setting. We want to set our business goals from a place of service and profit. We want to approach our businesses from a place of strategy, not emotion. Our emotions manifest when we set high-level goals. When setting weekly, monthly or yearly goals, we want to be able to look at it from a strategic perspective.

Many business owners in the first few years of business set their goals based on what they think they can do or what they feel they deserve instead of what is necessary for the business, its growth, reach and ultimately the best way to serve the client.

Personal Goals

We want to achieve things because of the way it makes us feel, not necessarily because of the achievement itself. It is important to step into the light of this awareness. Most of us want to feel loved, safe and secure. My question for you is, how can you obtain that feeling right here, right now? One way to do this is to focus on what is currently in your life that makes you feel loved, safe and secure.

Your personal financial goals will reflect your life path and the impact you are destined to make in the world. This is set from the heart rather than your head, allowing you to feel your way through, instead of letting fear, doubt or social pressures dictate your decisions. It will be easier to reach your targets as it is heart and soul-driven, with a purpose that is aligned to you, your values and your life's path.

Ensure that your goals are yours, not disguised expectations from friends, society, family, etc. Do you even want to have kids? Do you want to run a business? Start understanding your motives and the driving force behind your personal goals. This will provide momentum and encouragement to propel you when things get tough.

Money Blocks and Beliefs

Money beliefs manifest in our work, our relationship with others, our relationship with ourselves, and the way we think, feel and act. In today's world, we tend to judge people based on what they wear, how they walk, who they associate with, their residential area, where they socialise, what jobs they have, etc. Through these judgements, we knowingly or unknowingly estimate people's worth. These form the basis of what we think about the world and the role we play in it. Most times, we not only judge others' external worth, but also our internal worth.

These beliefs around our internal worth determine our perspective of the world—the way we see events and situations that happen to us and around us, the way we see our parents and people react to us, and the way we express ourselves in our lives and businesses. They also filter how we see opportunities that come our way.

Are we actually seeing the opportunies in front of us? Is our judgement so clouded that we do not see them at all? Or do we see an opportunity and not take it because we think it is too good to be true? Some people believe they are 'not ready' to accept certain opportunities. The truth is that opportunites do not only cross our path when we are ready; they may also come because we are ready to dismantle any old belief that contradicts it.

Before we go on, let us take a deeper look into some things. I mentioned the phrase 'the way we see things' a few times. We all exist from our perspectives, beliefs, our lives' chain of events, our upbringing and our culture.

Some money beliefs you may hold could look like these:

- I need to work hard for money
- I am a battler
- The underdog mentality
- I want to work with high-level clients
- Money is the root of all evil
- Money is power
- Money is not that important
- I am good with money

- The rich get richer, while the poor get poorer
- Money buys happiness
- Money makes life easy
- It is selfish to want a lot of money

If you are not in your desired financial position, here are some questions to ask yourself to learn about where your money beliefs and blocks lie:

- What did I hear and learn about money as a child?
- What do I make a lot of money mean to me?
- Who do I need to 'be' to get what I want?

Some months ago, I decided to rebrand my practice under my name instead of under a business name. I got my graphic designer to do a mood board for the new business. When I saw this mood board, I was quite taken back, as it looked so much better than how I felt at the time. So, I sat with it for a few days, and as I meditated on this, I realised it had everything to do with how I saw my self-worth. I wanted to expand my business and the quality my clients, but this also meant that I had to review my values, beliefs and standards. Through self-healing, I could release the blocks clouding my judgement. I realised that clients come to me because they cannot solve their problems by themselves, and they trust I have a solution. They are coming to me for my expertise. I removed the value I placed on the dollar and turned it into the energy exchange for services. Then, my mindset, my energy and my business levelled up.

Inherited Blocks and Beliefs

What are inherited money beliefs and blocks?

When referring to money, inherited beliefs are those beliefs, values, ideas, thoughts or feelings that do not come directly from us but from the influence of others. Most times, it comes directly from our parents during our earlier years. It can also come from the wider community; for example, aunts, uncles, mentors, teachers, media, etc. If your parents always focused on what they cannot afford, you may end up thinking from a place of lack. 70-80% of our beliefs is estimated to be established from upbringing, before the age seven.

These behavioural patterns from our younger years will influence our thoughts and beliefs on making money, as well as spending, saving, earning, investing, giving and receiving. They affect your beliefs and thoughts around people that have more or less money than you do, beliefs on how to feel, think and act around money—beliefs on how you think others perceive you in relation to money, which reflects your self-worth.

The more self-aware we become, the easier it gets to notice and identify our thoughts around money, but before this, our body and external world will let us know when there is something deeper to work on. Do conversations about money trigger certain emotions within you? Doubt, rejection, approval and faith in the future may be triggered by money talks. These emotions are associated with the spleen and stomach, hence the manifestation of health issues, such as food sensitivities, bloating, irritable bowel syndrome. You may also experience emotional manifestations in the form of disappointment, rejection, self-doubt, fear of criticism, uncertainty and anxiety about the future. These are all indicators that some belief changes need to be done around our relationship with money. Once they affect us on a physical level, we need to analyse both the physical and emotional causes as one can feed off the other.

LOVE IS WHAT WE ARE BORN WITH.
FEAR IS WHAT WE HAVE LEARNED HERE.
THE SPIRITUAL JOURNEY IS
THE UNLEARNING OF FEAR AND
THE ACCEPTANCE OF LOVE BACK
INTO OUR HEARTS.

—MARIANNE WILLIAMSON

PERSONAL

Here, we will explore self-love on a much deeper level, along with confidence, spirituality, fears and limiting beliefs. Some of these feelings reside in our subconscious without our awareness. However, our subconscious gives us physical and emotional clues through the way we feel, act and think. When we become more aware of our behaviours, we begin to observe these patterns and learn to decode them, to understand how they affect our lives and determine whether we want to make amends or not.

At the end of the day, we all have a choice to make. Yes, we have a choice. You get to decide whether to take the opportunity or not. To go out of your way to do the inner work, so that your outer world reflects your inner desires. The opportunities we see, the people we relate to and the way we see the world are reflections of what is happening on the inside, in our head, hearts and minds.

In a world where so many of us experience some form of anxiety or depression, it is evident that we have become a society that is disconnected from our feeling and from knowing what we personally need. It is time now to sit up, take note of how you feel and what your body is trying to tell you.

When your shoulders, chest, back, and legs are in pain, your body is talking to you about your path forward (see more in Part 2). When you are feeling resentful, hopeless, and distressed, it is important to listen to how you feel. Acknowledge what is happening within as this is your body and soul guiding you directly to the answers that lie within.

The more you work with your intuitive muscle, the more you will notice the guidance, understand it, and know that it has your back.

The easiest way to work with your intuitive muscle is to strip yourself of role play. From this standpoint, you can understand that there is no need for anxiety, there is no need for fear, and there is no need for self-judgement. There is only a need to experience love and joy, while creating from a place of purity and alignment.

Spirituality

As a child, I was exposed to so many different beliefs and faiths. Catholicism, Anglicanism, Jehovah Witness, Buddidsm, Judism, etc. Being exposed to different religions gave me the opportunity to explore them. They ignited my curiosity, so I had the opportunity to ask questions and delve into them a little deeper. Most of all, I loved hearing the stories from each faith. I noticed that while the stories were different, the themes were the same. They all seemed to give people a sense of hope. A sense of hope and belief in a higher force that is here to guide us along the way, to give us that understanding that we are never alone even if there are no other human beings around us. We can always connect with the universe.

I did not like reading until my mother gave me a book, Out on my Limb, by Shirley McClain. I remember thinking it was an old lady's book, but as I started reading it, I started falling in love. Her life journey, adventures and discoveries were relatable. Needless to say, I think I ended up reading most of her books. What I loved about these books was that they were not part of any religion, rather, they explored the essence of humanity. I understood that religion laid a foundation for better understanding of the world and self. Even now, some teachers and teachings resonate with me more than others. I see that as a sign of what I am ready to hear and learn in the present moment. It is not that one teacher is more right than another. It is more about what I am ready to process.

Your faith is a part of you. It helps you understand your connection to the universe, a connection worth exploring and nurturing. You will understand that you are never alone. I learnt to ask questions through prayer and receive clarity and guidance through meditation. This connection is always there to help us navigate through the ups and downs of life. It clarifies our confusions and eliminates the perspectives that blur our vision.

We have different spiritual experiences. Still, I urge you to look deeper and explore how you can incorporate spirituality into your life, something to give it a deeper meaning and connection.

Fears and Limiting Beliefs

We all have fears. Some of us are afraid of dying; some of us are afraid of spiders, the dark, or being attacked by a bear in the woods. Some of us have a fear of success or a fear of being in the spotlight; some of us have a fear of being wrong so we do not put ourselves out there. If we are not out there, we cannot receive criticism; we cannot be labelled wrong. But, it also puts a weight on our shoulders. Deep down, you know what you are here to do and the greatness you can achieve if you shift those fears even just a little.

Limiting beliefs complement fears. These are conscious and subconscious paradigms that govern our lives, passed down by our parents or instilled by life events. These limiting beliefs can be overcome and new ones installed in their place. We can change them, upgrade and improve any part of ourselves that we feel is holding us back. The truth is you can have, be and do anything you want. I have written this in a few places throughout this book so that it sinks in. You are a part of the greater universal energy. Your ability to create the life you desire is limited by your current thoughts and beliefs. Let us walk through those conscious and subconscious paradigms and get them to start working for you rather than against you. We can turn that hectic mountain climb into the feeling of floating above the clouds. You can have everything you need at your fingertips.

Self-Love

Self-love goes beyond learning to love and accept your body; it goes beyond giving yourself 'me time' to meditate, pampering yourself, and enjoying your own company. These things are external; they are things we 'do' to create that internal love, but self-love goes much deeper than that.

The deep, unconditional acceptance for oneself is the state we want to reside in. The love that says, I fully accept myself as a powerful being, that is not only unstoppable but also not afraid to be my true authentic self. The self that is not a parent, child, teacher, coach, and partner. The self that sits under those labels that we give ourselves. The one that sits under the empathy, the sensitive soul and the enlightened being. It is the pure essence of yourself you need to connect with and learn to unconditionally love and accept.

We are all connected by the energy around us, individualised by the body and perception of experiences we encounter on earth. We need to learn to fully accept who we are; mind, body, and spirit. To act from a place of total acceptance, gratitude and grace.

Part of self-love is the understanding that on this journey, there is a vast array of contrast. Ups and downs, good and bad—neither perspective holds the energy of wrong nor right. What is wrong can be right, and what is right can also be wrong, depending on the individual perspective and outlook. The question is, is your perspective working for you?

Through wholehearted acceptance of who we are, we can come to the place of unconditional love and acceptance, not only for ourselves but for others as well. From this perspective, we can understand that no one is right or wrong. We can determine which contrast works for us. 100% self-love attracts self-worth and self-acceptance, through which we will become truly unstoppable in life and business.

Confidence

Confidence is knowing that you have got this. That inner trust in yourself that everything will be okay no matter what the immediate outcome feels like. It is being okay with your limitations and knowing that you can seek help along the way. It is not only okay, it is an imperative part of business and life, be it your team helping you execute your business plans, a community of people that fully support one another, your family or your universal team—the collaboration with you and the universe. In every sphere of life, you are not alone. This deep knowing, trust and connection provide the confidence you need to take that next step forward.

No matter what level of business you are on, you are not here to do 100% of it on your own. Even as a solopreneur, there is always outsourcing to be done. We were never meant to be creatures of independence to the point of feeling alone and isolated. We are all part of a community that strives and thrives together. If you are feeling lost and disconnected, it is an internal sign that you are not doing life that way you want to, which is with connection. Connection is a core need, and when it is lost, it needs to be re-established. Connection goes beyond the social media connection that many of us are addicted to.

When you are travelling on your path, confidence helps you take that next step, to take that risk. To help you confront your fears and chase your demons, to help you grow personally and, therefore, in business. The confidence to know that every challenge, no matter how big or small, presents an opportunity to heal and grow into a better version of self, producing better, greater and more profound results for not only ourselves but for the wider community through our business.

Without confidence, life can start to feel stagnant. You may feel like you are on a hamster wheel because you are always second-guessing yourself. Therefore, you never take a step forward, or you take a step forward and run back, hoping that no one saw you. Running away in fear is running away from who you truly are and running away from the beautiful life waiting for you on the other side of fear.

Remember, true confidence stems from being aligned and living from your true authentic self, living life your way, on your terms, and living your true life's purpose—from following your internal guidance system, your emotions and your energy. When you use your internal GPS, you can be confident that you are on the right path. Life is always meant to feel good.

Purpose

Your purpose is what you would like to experience right now in this lifetime. It is about the life you would like to lead, the person you would like to be, who you want to be around, and the experiences you would like to have. Your purpose helps you navigate your life path. It is about what you are doing, who are you being right now and ensuring it is in alignment with what you want moving forward.

I saw this very clearly after exiting the fashion industry. I did not see my experience in the fashion industry as a total waste of time. I saw it as a continuation of my journey. I needed to go through that period to learn, grow and understand myself. At that time, if I were more aware of myself and followed my emotional GPS, I would have made that transition four years earlier, when I lost my passion. Anxiety set in and my body was breaking down. Now, I look back and see this as a personal lesson of connecting with myself and acknowledging what is going on, what my emotions were trying to tell me.

On some level, whether we are conscious about it or not, we all want to experience unconditional love. To experience unconditional love, we must also experience the opposite. This would help us grow and recognise that it is unconditional love we desire. If we do not experience fear and the discomfort that comes with it, how do we know what we would prefer instead? We may need to experience something that we do not want to recognise and ask ourselves what we do want.

Experiencing the depth of what does not feel good acts as a propeller to push us in the direction that does feel good, if we recognise where we are. Many of us sit in the discomfort for too long and can start to feel too powerless to move forward. Once we come to the realisation of where we are and how it feels, we are empowered to choose the next step forward.

If you are unsure about what this may be for you, you can start by exploring your current state and asking yourself, 'Is what I am experiencing where I want to be?' If not, what is it teaching you? Our desires extend a lot further than us; for example, when I look back at the some experinces I have had, the importance of self-healing is distinct. I now understand the need for others to heal through whatever life has given them. I know that part of my purpose is to not only learn to heal through my own experiences, but part of my life's path is to help others do exactly the same.

Your personal journey will somehow connect to your life's path. When you take a step out of the emotions currently consuming you, you can see your life from a slightly different perspective. It is through this objective perspective that we can clearly see where we are and have a better understanding of how to get to where we want to be. It helps us to consciously create our path forward with more ease and flow.

Your purpose drives you forward when times are tough. It helps you remember why you are on your current path and gives you a solid foundation.

WE ARE NOT VICTIMS,
WE ARE THE CREATORS.
IF WE PUT STRESS IN OUR LIVES
THEN WE MANIFEST DISEASE.
IF WE REMOVE STRESS FROM OUR LIVES,
WE CAN REMOVE DISEASE.

—DR. BRUCE LIPTON

HEALTH

What do you need to live your full, abundant life? We have been given these beautiful bodies to experience life with. How do we look after it?

Firstly, we must learn to listen to our bodies, understand what it is trying to tell us and respect it. Very few of us have learnt to do all three, or even come to the awareness that sending some love and focus within improves the quality our life. When we learn to listen to the way we feel, physically, mentally, and emotionally, and respect ourselves by living our personal values and beliefs with boundaries around them, we thrive.

We are often led to believe that putting ourselves first is a selfish act. We are expected to give others our best when our cup is not even half full. When we put ourselves first, providing our mind, body and soul with the nourishment they require, we are placed in a better position to help others because we are not giving from a depleted cup.

It is important to remember that our body function depends on balance. When we are emotionally off, we are also physically and mentally out, which will affect other areas of our life and business. We cannot work on one area in isolation. There are five health pillars that need to be nutured for you to attain your ultimate self. They are:

Physical Health: Nutrition, Movement, Activity, Environmental Toxins.

Mental Health: Emotions, Relationships, Self-Talk.

Mind-Body Connection: To build an understanding between what you are physically feeling, your emotions and your beliefs that are being triggered.

Healing Path: Your selection of tools and modalities to assist you in your self-care.

Effects on your Business/Career: The awareness of what we are currently doing is impacting other areas of life.

Your body is the vehicle that carries you through life. It is important to give it the servicing and nurturing it needs. A great question to ask yourself is, what does my body need to perform at optimal level? Emotionally, you may feel fear, anxiety, frustration and confidence. If you are experiencing any of these, you may need to feel and explore those feelings a little deeper.

Mental Clarity

Mental health is the foundation of our mental clarity. The way we think and feel determines how we act. Do you often find yourself sitting in a negative headspace, stressed, or are you feeling refreshed, clear and alive? Are you ready to face life and all its lessons, or are you cringing at the possibility of more issues?

Many of us go through our lives feeling disconnected from who we are because we are so busy playing the role of the mother, wife, business owner, supporter, healer, rescuer, or victim. We get so caught up playing these roles that we forget how to come back to ourselves. This is when anxiety, depression, and overwhelm set in. Our mental clarity helps us make the best decisions in our life and business. We cannot make the best decisions when are head is clouded and overloaded with to-dos, schedules, emotions, fears and worries. You need to learn to operate with a clear mind and notice what the mind is saying to itself, that is, self-observation. When we operate from the self-observation mode, we learn to disconnect from the emotions and navigate life smoother.

When we have a computer, its memory can start to get full and ends up flashing up a dialogue window with a warning that we need to start to clear some files. If you continually ignored this message, your computer will not only have trouble doing the normal tasks, but it will eventually wont be able to take any more. It will not close a program or open or delete files. If you leave it long enough, it can even struggle to reboot.

Guess what! You are no different. Sometimes, we fill our bodies and minds with toxic thoughts, feelings and substances, beyond tolerable levels. When our minds are full of data, we start to get snappy and overwhelmed. Anxiety sets in, depression rises, and we can mentally breakdown. This is our personal dialogue window pop-up. This affects our clarity and physical body. We start to make irrational and even reckless decisions from this place of stress and anxiety. When it is time to reboot, reset and crawl out of this space, we are so exhausted and lost, barely knowing where to begin.

It is important to check what you grant access into your mind. What are you watching? Are the conversations you are having feeding you positively or negatively? What are you subconsciously listening to when the radio plays in the background? All of this has an impact on the way you mentally process everything and, therefore, your everyday clarity of thought.

Physical Health

Physical health entails how we nourish our physical bodies. The foods we eat, the liquids we drink, medication, recreational drugs, etc. Are you consuming the right variety and amount of nutrients?

When we talk about energy, we talk about our Qi/Prana of the body, our inner life force. This includes the energy our bodies need to think, feel and move and what our internal organs need to function. Using up this energy for the digestion of heavy foods inhibit other activities within the body. Have you ever been tired after a big bowl of pasta? Sometimes, all you want to do is sleep it off, as you do not have energy for anything else. This can also happen on a subtler level.

We know through many studies that aerobic exercises increase the level of oxygen in the body, which helps balance out our hormones. It increases our serotonin levels (one of the 'happy hormones'). We not only feel better, but our body is also more balanced, and we are mentally clearer.

With exercise, I do have a word of warning: It can work against your mental health. Yes, I said that. As I mentioned earlier, exercise helps us think and feel better by activation of certain chemicals. What it does not do is solve our problems for us. I have seen people use exercise as a self-medication tool without addressing the real underlying problems. Clearing your head and looking inwards helps. This is why I recommend a mediation/reflection session after exercise. Never ignore your problems or attempt to coat them with things like exercise, food, alcohol, drugs, sex, work, etc. They will always resurface and may even hit harder than before.

In my early 20s, I exercised almost every day. This was my way of energising my mind and body, a coping mechanism to prepare me for the day's activities. But, I did not realise I was not doing any further self-care; I discarded negativity with exercise and because the exercise made me feel better in my mind, there was no need to address the problem anymore.

If the problem resurfaced, I would exercise again, and the cycle continued. I did not realise that the exercise would only suppress my emotions while they manifested as physical discomfort within my body. This was the beginning of my fructose malabsorption. I now understand that exercise can be very beneficial, but it has to be done properly. When we understand our state of being, we can use exercise to move out of that state and gain clarity.

Life speaks to us on three levels:

Level One: Feather

This is our intuition or gut instinct. It speaks to us softly, like a whisper. This is the stage a lot of people miss. They are too focused on the external rather than connecting to the peace and quite of their internal, which has all the answers we need. When we learn to trust and act on our intuition, we will notice that it has a lot to say. Open your lines of communication and establish a friendship with yourself. You will notice just how accurate and knowledgeable you are.

Level Two: Brick

This is where things hit us a bit harder in the hope that we will take a little more notice of what is happening. It is our inner guidance that chats with us through our thoughts, feelings and emotions. When we feel the discomfort of emotions through stress and anxiety, it is our emotional guidance system at work.

Level Three: Truck

Sometimes, we may be so caught up with life, we miss all the previous signs. This is when life throws a truck on our path. This is the physical pain, discomfort and dis-ease. We are forced to sit up, take note and take action to move away from pain and back into pleasure. The goal is to avoid getting to stage three. However, some of us need the extreme discomforts that life throws our way to acknowledge the contrast between where we are and where we want to be. This helps us make rapid changes in our lives and get back on track.

It is not always about the action taken, but also about the learning process. Consider the lessons presented by the different scenarios of your life. A deeper sense of self-awareness is always going to be the first step of your healing journey.

Mind and Body Connection

The connection you have with you body is able to give you so much feedback and can provide so much emotional clarity and self-realisation. The profound messages and guidance provided by our mind and body help us move forward on our life's journey. Yes, this book will help guide you, but your biggest guide will be you and the way you feel. Honour your feeling every moment of every day and ensure you feel good. One step better than good is to feel exactly the way you want to feel.

A few years ago, I lost my unborn daughter 20 weeks into my pregnancy. After that, I felt the urge to sit in grief and sadness for six days. This was my processing time. I can still recall the moment I knew it was time to take the next step forward. There is a distinction between honouring the way you feel and letting your emotions take over. When our emotions instigate negativity, we start to impact the world within and around us. This is a good indication to start looking at some sort of healing process to help you work through the emotions, acknowledge them, learn and grow through the experience.

When we are travelling through life, holding on to our emotions for a prolonged period, the energy of these emotions will start to build up within our physical body. As I mentioned in the previous chapter, Physical Health, this happens through chemical imbalances. Clinging to unwanted emotions will cause emotional, mental and physical imbalances. A lot of people have never been taught this. You need to be aware of the physical pains you endure, resulting from unchecked emotions, especially those small aches that we have learnt to put up with for so long that it has become difficult to identify the origin behind these thought patterns and accumulated energies. (See Part two for more).

Depression affects the large intestine. Hence, we find that a lot of people with depression can have some sort of gut imbalance. When we look at this, and how it plays out in our reality, we look at disconnection from self and others, in the form of ineffective communication, which also manifests in the marketing aspects of business.

Healing Path

I like to look at this as a big part of our conscious creation. It is about taking full, unconditional ownership of ourselves and where we are currently at in life and knowing who you are and there for and where you want to be going forward to.

When we look at our life and blame others for who we feel, the situations that awe are in and what has happened to us, we give away part of our power. The power that has the ability to create change. The part of us that gets to say how we want to feel and when.

This is why part of our healing needs to be forgiveness. This is never about condoning any situation, it actually has nothing to do with anyone else. Forgivness is about releasing the emotion from the even and giving you back the rights and decision on where you wan to move forward to from here.

To create the future you want, you need to create the now that you want. Take full responsibility for how you feel, what you think, what you do, who you are and what direction you want to go in. From here you can sit with all the discomforts as they arise which is the perfect start to your healing journey. There is always some 'gold' learning in these discomforts, and when released, the forward flow of life will lead you right into the hands of your desires, long your perfectly aligned life path.

The healing path is not only about the way we think and feel but the entirety of our whole life. Learn to enjoy the healing journey; it has so many great lessons about the depth of who we are. We can shift the perspectives of our past, present and future to unleash our true power.

I started this journey when I was diagnosed with fructose malabsorption. I thought that if I was not born with this, I should be able to heal it. I learnt about my thought process and what it was doing to the way I was physically feeling. Before deep-diving further into the healing modality, I had no idea that we could change the way we are. I thought that I was just a stressful person, and I would have to learn to deal with that. A lot of us learn to deal with our discomforts when we do not have to. What we do not understand is that if something does not feel right, it is not right, and it can be changed. You can swap behaviours that do not feel right, for ones that feel right. It is a matter of choice. This applies to misaligned emotions as well.

I experienced this deeply when I went through my miscarriage. I felt so many deep, painful emotions day after day—I did not know where to turn. Even with all my tools that I had used in the past and all the support that I had, I found it difficult to scale through. One day, I was lying in my hospital bed sobbing uncontrollably when I felt this profound shift come over me. It was like a movie playing in real-time. I had never experienced anything like it before. I saw every problem that I thought I had from previous days, weeks, years and even decades, disappear emotionally in one second.

For some reason, I was so consciously aware throughout this experience. I could see the emotional shift that was taking place. It stopped me in its tracks, not from the pain that I was currently experiencing, but from the realisation that previous pain could disappear in seconds. I believe there was an energy shift. We are where our focus is, and at that point, 100% of my energy was focused on the present time. Therefore, all the past hurt and pain were automatically released. Goind forward, I became conscious of emotional pain and baggage. I can clearly see now that we have a choice whether we want to carry them with us or not. You are able to shift your focus and let them go.

Effects on Business

We can create desirable effects in our lives with the awareness of who we are and how we feel. We know that what we think, feel and do play a huge role in the physical outcome of life. Not only in our personal life but in our business as well. One of my mentors once said, 'There is no separation between you and your business.'

Our fears, limiting beliefs and anxieties will always manifest in our life and our business. They may present with slight variation, but the underlying cause remain the same.

As entrepreneurs, the journey through starting, growing and scaling a business is no different from a personal development journey. In fact, it is a personal development journey. We discover thoughts, feelings and inner limitations that we did not know we had, and at the same time, we find strength, knowledge and talents that we never knew existed. Embrace the highs and lows of business with curiosity, knowing it will lead you to a fully balanced life as you heal. In every turn of life, there is always an opportunity to learn and grow. As you grow so does your business.

Through my business journey, I now understand that the disconnection I had with myself, the disconnection I had with my partner and the feeling of social anxiety not only affect me but also the results I got in my business. My aim in business is to help and empower as many people as possible. The understanding of importance self empowerment is, is a massive driver for me to work on myself and become a better person, so I can serve from my authentic self and from my pure zone of genius. Working through my disconnection strengthened my relationships with my friends and family as well as my clients and wider audience.

This is what I want for you—to empower you in the knowledge that you have full control over the direction of your life, your business and their outcomes. I want to empower you with the knowledge that you have everything within you to succeed. Understanding what your body is telling you about your life and your business is one of the most empowering knowledge that I have encountered. Now, I hand it over to you to continue your journey. The next part of this book will give more detail on this.

You will learn to understand what your body is telling you about your life and your business, to shift your awareness, and therefore, shift your trajectory.

PART 2

Reference Section—By Governing House

Welcome to part two, where I have outlined everything you need to know about the mental and physical pain that you may be holding. Before we begin, you should know that this is only a part of your journey. If the pain has existed for a prolonged time, you may need medical intervention; for example, Naturopath, Chinese Medicine Practitioner, Acupuncturist, Kinesiologist, general practitioner or another specialist.

This section has been designed as your go-to guide to understanding yourself and what your body is trying to tell you about your life and your business. By now, you should understand that you have everything you need to heal, grow and thrive. However, you may not know how to decode what your body is telling you. What does it mean when we feel emotional pain? What does it mean when we feel physical pain and are the physical and emotional pains connected? Some of us have been taught that there is only a physical side to life, the material posessions and what we can see is all there is. When we explore deeper both in science and in our hearts, we know there is much much more. The next pages will empower you with the consciousness of choice. You will be aware of what you are feeling, and gain a deeper insight to help you release the stagnant energy around your pain and discomfort.

There are many emotions, emotional responses and reactions that we experience throughout our life. Most of these emotions reside in certain muscles, which means that when we feel muscular pain, we can determine the emotion stored there, release them and relieve the pain. Feel free to look up the emotion that you are experiencing or where the physical pain is located.

What mental stress or emotions do you feel? Where is the physical pain that you are experiencing?

I have noticed times within myself and within my clients that coming to the pure awareness around why we are experiencing pain or discomfort is enough within itself to release the energy of the pain. Sometimes, more work is required. We are all different and require different things. This is why, within my practice, I have over 50 methods to rebalance your energy.

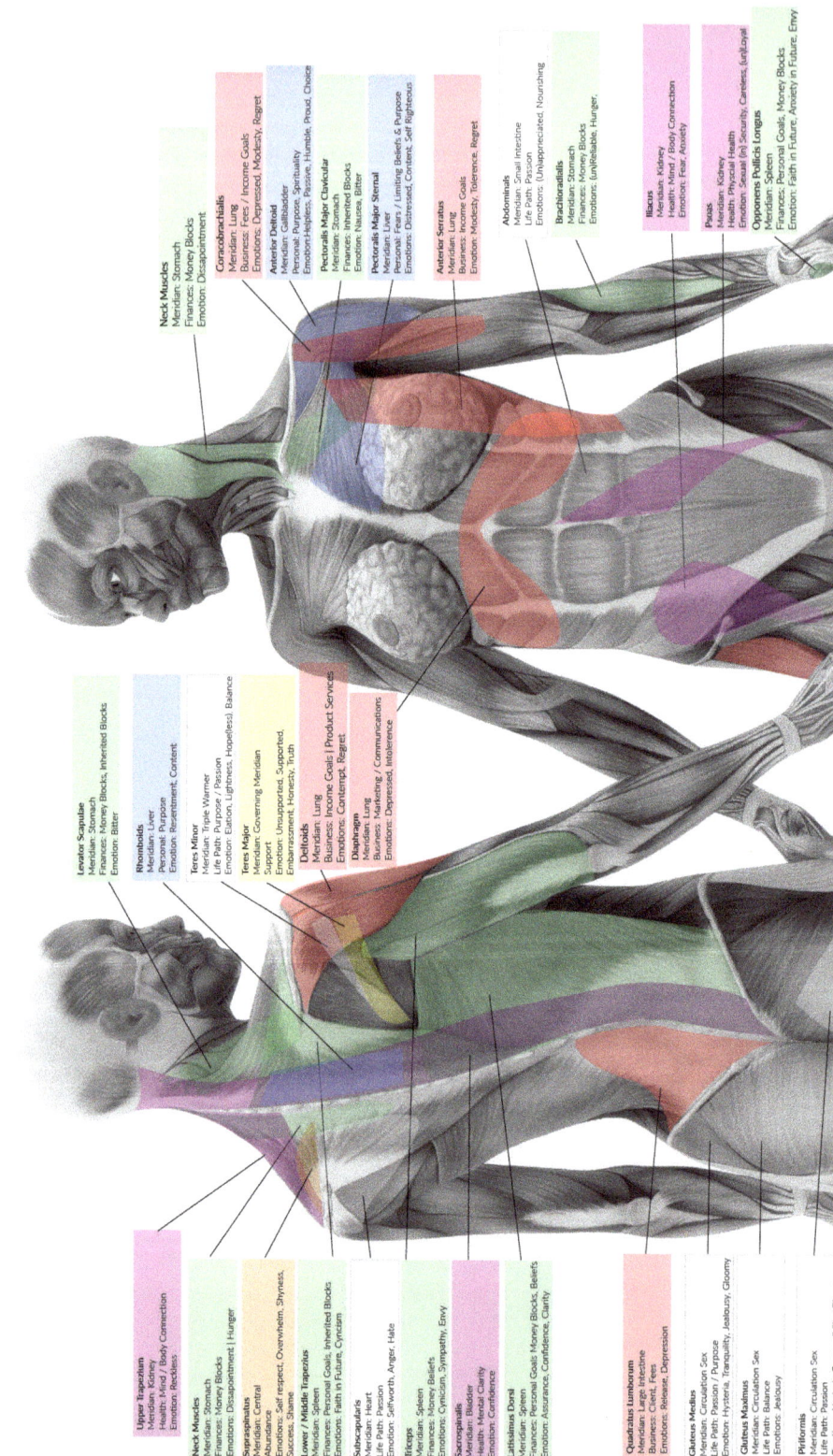

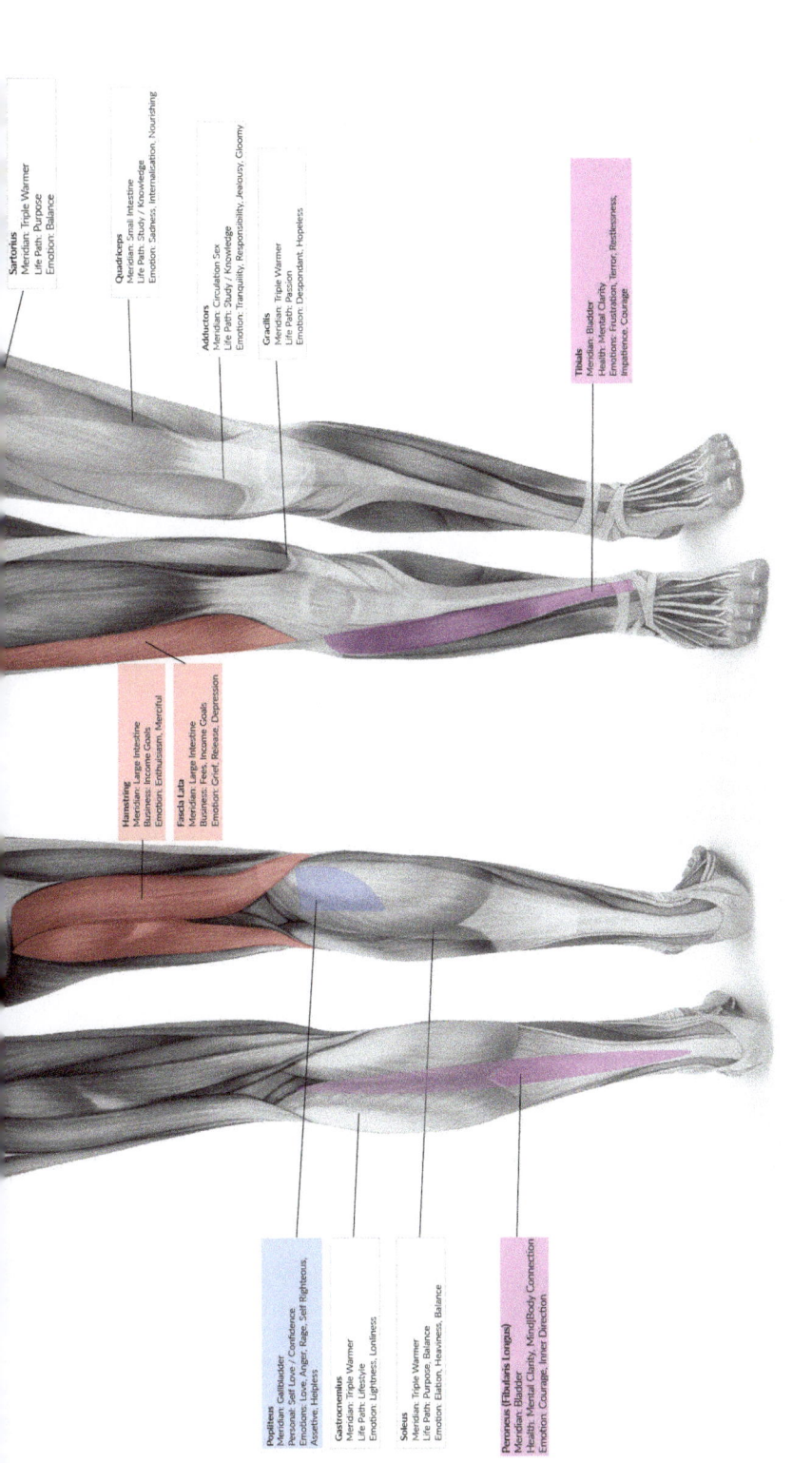

IN SEPARATIONS,
LIES THE WORLD'S GREATEST SUFFERING.
IN UNITY,
LIES THE WORLD'S TRUE STRENGTH.

—BUDDHA

FOUNDATION

Associated Emotions

Self-Respect, Overwhelm, Shyness, Success, Shame, Embarrassment, Unsupported, Supported, Honesty, Truth

Affected Muscles

Supraspinatus, Teres Major

Teres Major

Yang Energy

Health: Support

Emotions: Unsupported, Supported, Embarrassment, Honesty, Truth

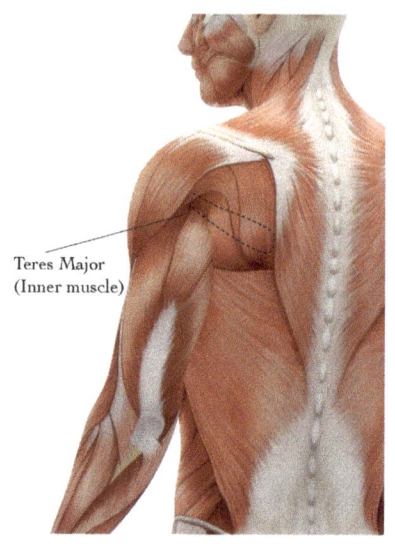

Teres Major (Inner muscle)

When we start to feel unsupported in life and business, it is because we have deviated from our life paths. You may feel resentful, unmotivated and stagnant (procrastination).

We may feel like there is a missing piece of ourselves or the bigger puzzle. A deeper connection to self is that missing piece. When we realign and go down our unique path once more, we realise that we are not alone and that we have every support that is needed, both from the universe and those around us.

The is the same for when we feel like we are supporting others and not receiving it back in return. It is not their job to support us and not ours to support them. Support needs to originate from within. External support should be knowledge and task-based, not emotional support that keeps us motivated. While it is important to learn to hold space while other process their emotions, beware of signs of needing external validation. If you find yourself constantly needing emotional support from others, you may need to do some self-exporation.

Questions to help spark your inner awareness

What are you currently doing in business that feels heavy and is not congruent with who you really are and what you want to stand for?

Do you feel disconnected from who you are?

Are you wanting others to approve of you? What are you really looking for here?

If you said yes to the above, are the people around you on the same path as you?

Supraspinatus

Yin Energy

Health: Abundance

Emotions: Self-respect, Overwhelm, Shyness, Success, Shame

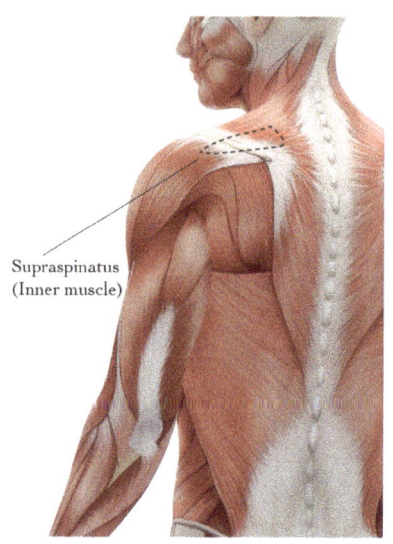
Supraspinatus (Inner muscle)

Your vision in business may be unclear due to overwhelm or procrastination.

These muscles and emotions are triggered when we have an over-accumulation of emotions that have been pushed aside and stored in our physical body. Whether we consciously know that they are there or not, our body knows and will let you know through this muscle and emotions.

Remind yourself here, that you are naturally an abundant magnetic being. You don't have to work hard for this.

Co-creating with the universe is how you travel on your path to the desired desitination. Most of the time the universe will give you one step at a time.

Questions to help spark your inner awareness

What small actions can you take today, that will lead you to the next step?

What part of you are you trying to protect with the way you currently see yourself and the world?

What is holding you back from having everything you want?

CREATE THE HIGHEST,
GRANDEST VISION POSSIBLE FOR
YOUR LIFE,
BECAUSE YOU BECOME WHAT
YOU BELIEVE.

—OPRAH WINFREY

LIFE PATH

Associated Emotions

Joy, Sorrow, Sadness, Appreciated, Underappreciated, Overexcited, Internalisation, Assimilation, Nourishing, Despair, Elation, Despondent, Lightness, Heaviness, Loneliness, Humiliated, Hope(less), Serving, Balance, Forgiveness, Self-esteem, Self-worth, Insecure, Secure, Anger, Hate, Love, Calm, hysteria, Relaxation, Stubbornness, Tranquillity, Responsible, Jealousy, Remorse, Gloomy.

Affected Muscles

Subscapularis, Quadricepts, Abdominals, Gluteus Medius, Adductors, Piriformis, Gluteus Maximus, Teres Minor, Sartorius, Gracilis, Soleus, Gastrocnemius

Gluteus Medius

Yin Energy

Life Path: Passion, Purpose

Emotions: Hysteria, Jealousy, Gloomy, Tranquility

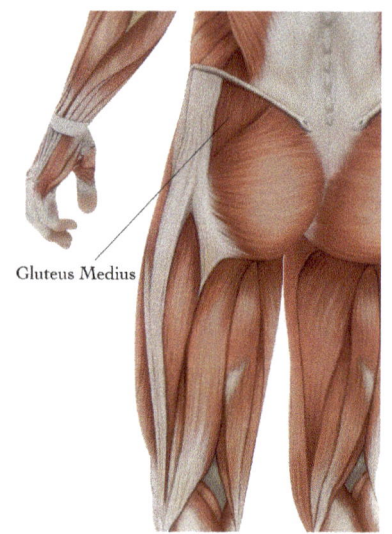
Gluteus Medius

To reignite your sense of purpose and passion, think about what you stand for and the impact you want to create. As much as it it nice to have a 10year vision, sometimes it is about what you want to achieve this week or this year. We cannot work on the small daily tasks unless we know where it is leading.

Plan it out before taking action and trust yourself along the way. Trust the guidance that you are given from within when you have clarity for where you are going and boundaries paving that path around it. This way things will fall into place with more ease and flow.

This will ensure your internal alignment when executing short-term goals.

Questions to help spark your inner awareness

Are you giving too much attention to the little details and not getting enough clarity about the bigger picture, and why you want the big picture to become a reality?

Or

Are you too focused on the bigger picture and cannot see how to get there?

Adductors

Yin Energy

Life Path: Study, Knowledge

Emotions: Tranquillity, Responsibility, Jealousy, Gloomy

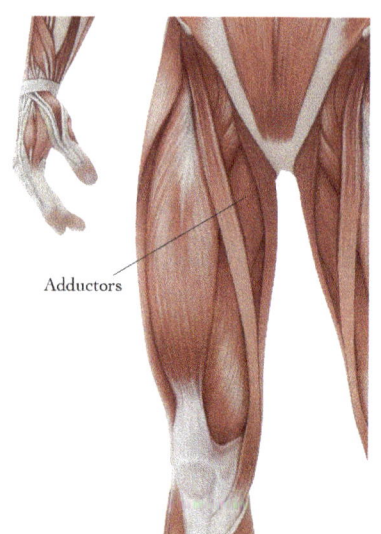
Adductors

When it comes to our gifts and utilising them within our careers, we need to work out what information we need to keep to ourselves and what serves the world to share.

Are you 100% comfortable in your career and knowledge that you have been given to work with and share, or are you holding back?

This is about communication with self. It is that internal chatter about who you are and what you bring to your career. Is it positive and uplifting, or is it filled with doubt and fear of been seen, fear of not being good enough?

Questions to help spark your inner awareness-

What knowledge are you keeping private? What about yourself, do you not want people to know?

Does it feel good to communicate what you do with everyone around you? Or do you feel the need not to tell some people some things? Why?

Piriformis

Ying Energy

Life Path: Passion

Emotions: Hysteria, Responsibility, Gloomy

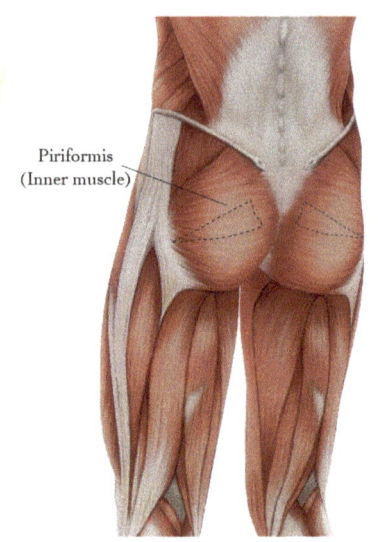

Do you feel pressure and an overwhelming sense of responsibility to provide from your career? This lowers the energy around your passion for work and life.

The stagnant energy in this muscle will cause a push-pull effect, which influences decisions that you make within your business and work.

This muscle is related to impaired external communication (with others) and fear of making the wrong decisions.

Releasing the energy around what you perceive as 'responsibility' and the old beliefs around this will present a newfound clarity and momentum.

Questions to help spark your inner awareness-

Is there pressure on your work to provide?

Are you trying too hard to make things work?

How can you release this pressure?

Gluteus Maximus

Yin Energy

Life Path: Balance

Emotions: Jealousy

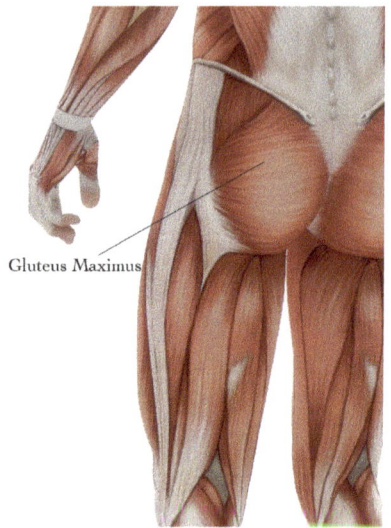

When we push too hard to obtain result in our business, we execute from our headspace and disconnect from the heart. Alternatively, you may be sitting in your heart for too long and not take any action.

This muscle can be imbalanced when we execute life and business from either our heart or our heads rather than from a place of balance. This is where the masculine and feminine balance in business really shows up. (Feminine = creative, flow, ideas, receiving. Masculine = strategy, action, giving)

It is important here to be guided by service and passion rather than only by results.

Remember your 'why' vision and your customer when you take action in your business.

Questions to help spark your inner awareness

Are you sitting too much in your head and not enough in your heart?

Or

Are you sitting too much in your heart and not connecting with your potential clients?

Are you using too much strategy and not enough creative connection and meaning?

Teres Minor

Yang Energy

Life Path: Purpose, Passion

Emotions: Elation, Lightness, Hopeless, Balance

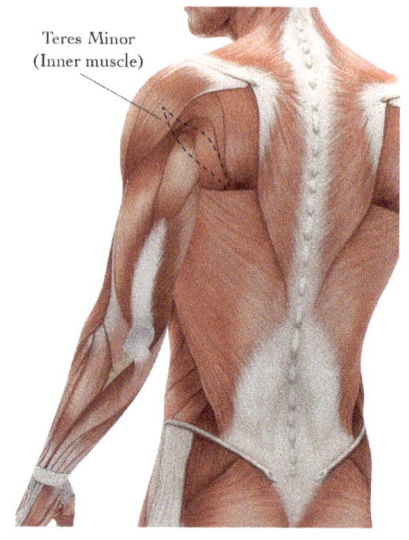

Is there a part of you that is either too closed off or too open?

Gently open up to receiving and do not take things too hastily. Allow the flow to occur in your life. The flow of information, resources, money, appreciation and love.

Be careful not to shut down people or ideas too quickly. Slow down your energy a bit, so you can give and receive freely.

Push-pull emotion imbalance here can cause you to experience extreme feelings, emotions, passion and action—from being too rushed hot-headed and irrational to freezing up and either not taking any action at all or doing the actions that you feel you 'should' be doing. Not the actions that are in alignment with where you are right now.

Give yourself the opportunity here to pause and re-evaluate to be able to proceed in an aligned mindful way.

Questions to help spark your inner awareness

Is there a part of you that is either too closed off or too open?

Is there an aspect of life where you are receiving harsh treatment?

Are your emotions up and down? One minute soft and gentle and harsh the next?

Gracilis

Yang Energy

Life Path: Passion

Emotions: Despondent, Hopeless

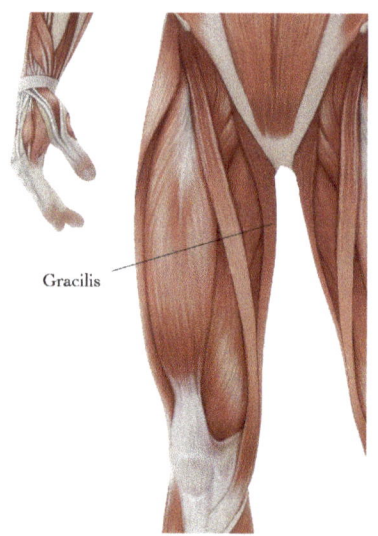

Questions to help spark your inner awareness

Are you so enthusiastic about your passion that your judgment on how to move forward is clouded?

Do you need to learn how to bring the bigger picture into a calm, centred place, so that the forward steps reveal themselves and become clearer to you, enabling you to walk your path with ease and flow?

Or

Does your passion make you nervous because you are afraid to share it with the world for fear of being ridiculed or not feeling good enough?

These internal fears hinder your progress, self-expression, communication and knowledge.

It is extremely important to remember your 'why' and only focus on your customer that needs and wants to hear your message.

Switch the focus here from yourself to your consumer.

Soleus

Yang Energy

Life Path: Purpose, Balance

Emotions: Elation, heaviness, Balance

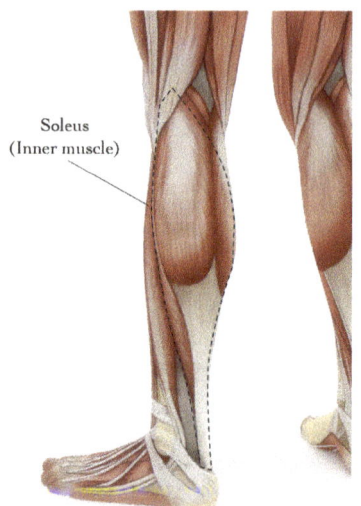

This muscle is about finding balance with our expression within you business.

It becomes over energised when we are in a consistent tug of war, when we express ourselves from the head and instead of the heart. The long-term effect of this is the feeling of being unsupported by life and the people around you as they don't understand the direction you are going in. When you are holding back it then affects the level of abundance that flows into your life.

It is important to establish balance between fighting for what you are passionate about and holding back. To find that conscious connection with ourselves and our work, where our message simply flows from the heart and the head is there to support us.

Questions to help spark your inner awareness

How confortable are you with expressing your purpose to both yourself and the people around you?

Are you censoring yourself?

Gastrocnemius

Yang Energy

Life Path: Lifestyle

Emotions: Lightness, Loneliness

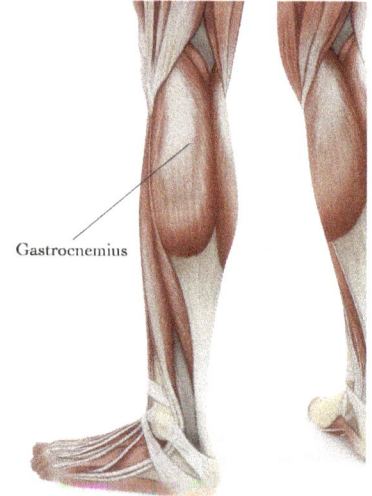

This is about the inability to make decisions and difficulty in figuring out how to get the life you desire through your career. It can result in procrastination and exhausting all your energy on your business, sparing none for your personal life or the inspiration for other ideas. Your personal life and business may be at conflict with eachother with no real progress in either. You many find one progressing and the other stagnant with no way to figure out how to do both at once. This happens when we push things to happen instead of sitting in our flow and allowing.

There is an inability to move forward because of this internal conflict. This is a great time for clarity and self-reflection. You may even consult someone else to bring in fresh perspectives. Loneliness is the associated emotion with this muscle, hence, a trusting partner, friend, business mentor or therapist can be a great support here.

This muscle is often over energised when we push and try and do too much, and is under energised when we sit in procrastitation and do not execute enough. In both instances you are trying to do it alone. Reaching out for that external perspective here will help immensely.

Questions to help spark your inner awareness

Are you living the lifestyle that you innately desire?

Is there balance between your personal life and your business?

What adjustments can you make for things to add up?

Are you pushing to much to obtain the lifestyle that you want, but actually moving futher away?

Subscapularis

Yin Energy

Life Path: Passion

Emotions: Self-worth, Anger, Love

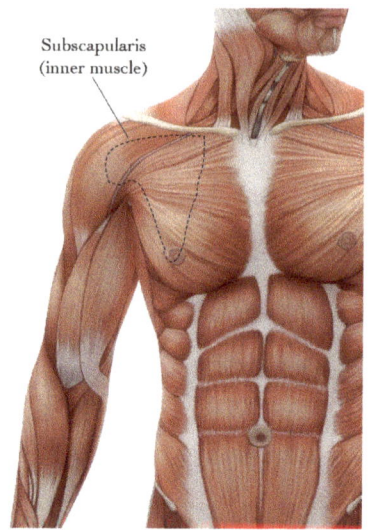

There may be certain important people you have locked out of your life. This happens when we forget to acknowledge that we are energetic beings that attract like energy. These people and situations have been brought in to mirror to you parts of yourself that need to be healed.

Do not filter who you are or worry about others' acceptance of you. Connect to your heart space with all the trust that this is exactly where you are meant to be. Others will see the passion ignite within you and those who need to be a part of your tribe will have the opportunity to connect with you. Your authenticity is your filter.

If you close your heart down to one person, you close off growth, future opportunities and the flow of abundance.

Move forward with your heart open, and you will bring that you need and desire through the experiences into your life.

Questions to help spark your inner awareness

Are you closing off your true gifts and passion?

Are you selecting who you bring in and who you let out, instead of allowing your energy to be the automatic filter that it is?

Or

Are you giving out too much and not giving enough to yourself?

Do you need to bring in better boundaries?

Quadriceps

Yang Energy

Life Path: Study, Knowledge

Emotions: Sadness, Internalisation, Nourishing

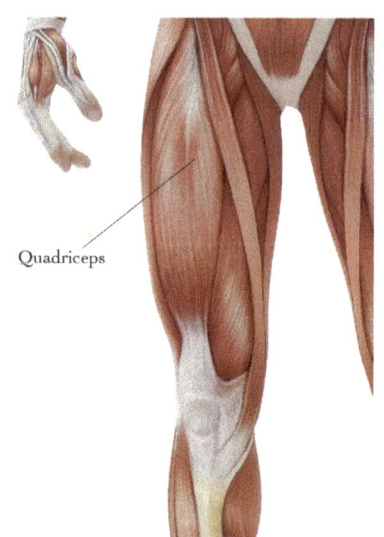

Quadriceps

It can be unbalancing to start taking action on goals that require new knowledge and learning without having clarity on what the outcome will be.

When we internalise our thoughts and feelings or excessively work from an emotional place, we may feel like life is happening to us.

Once we stop, plan and gain clarity about our forward direction, we can obtain the skill, knowledge and understanding required to direct our future from a heartfelt place. Sometimes, you only need to see the NEXT step. When you take that step, the one after that will reveal itself. Not knowing too much can be our greatest asset and can shield us from overwhelm.

Questions to help spark your inner awareness

Does your forward plan feel too big that you do not know how to step forward?

Or

Do you have ambiguous goals?

Are you unsure of your next move?

What can you do to bring forward clarity on your next step.

Abdominals

Yang Energy

Life Path: Passion

Emotions: (un) Appreciated, Nourishing

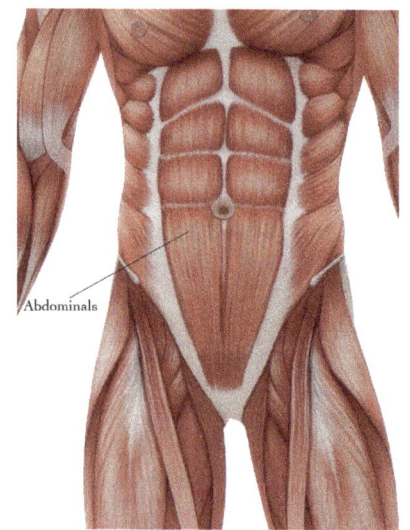

There are times in business where there are tasks to do that can feel less important, but you know still needs to be done. Sometimes they feel mundane but you can also see how they make the business function.

Do you feel like your daily tasks place you on the right path or do you feel like they are distracting you from reaching and building momentum on your forward path in life and business? It is time to weigh your options, either you fully appreciate the execution of these tasks or you outsource.

Questions to help spark your inner awareness

What are you doing in your business that is holding you back from sitting nicely in your zone of genius?

How is your attitude towards roles/tasks in your business?

What tasks are you not like doing?

Is your business feeling like a chore?

Sartorius

Yin Energy

Life Path: Purpose

Emotions: Balance

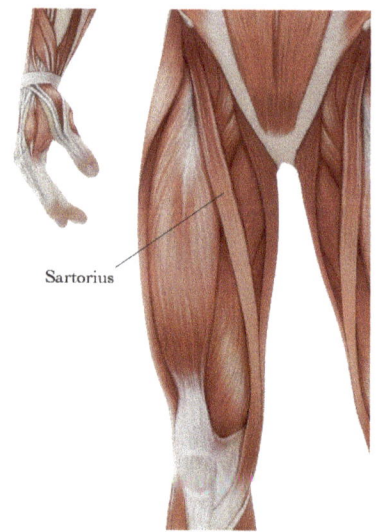

This muscle is thrown out of balance when you feel the pressure of trying to obtain the balance that we desire in life and business. being over consumped by work and feel as though you are missing out on life. This consistent pressure can start to diminish your sense of purpose. It is important to understand that there is no limit to reaching for your goals. Once one goal is obtained, there is a better quality one to replace it with, so obtaining that balance you desire during the growth process is very important.

Questions to help spark your inner awareness

Are you feeling out of balance and consumed by your work?

Do you have the passion to guide you through tougher seasons?

THE SIMPLE FACT IS,
IF YOU DON'T TAKE CARE OF YOURSELF,
YOU WON'T BE ABLE TO TAKE CARE
OF BUSINESS.

—RICHARD BRANSON

BUSINESS

Associated Emotions

Cheerful, Depressed, False pride, Haughty, Humility|Modesty, Scorn|Distain, (in)Tolerance, Prejudice, Contempt, Regret, Guilt, Grief, Regret, Self-worth, Enthusiasm, Depression, Letting go, Indifference, (un)Merciful, Apathy, Release

Affected Muscles

Anterior Serratus, Coracobrachialis, Deltoid, Diaphram, Fascia Lata, Hamstring, Quad. Lumborum

Anterior Serratus

Yin Energy

Business: Income Goals

Emotions: Modesty, Tolerance, Regret

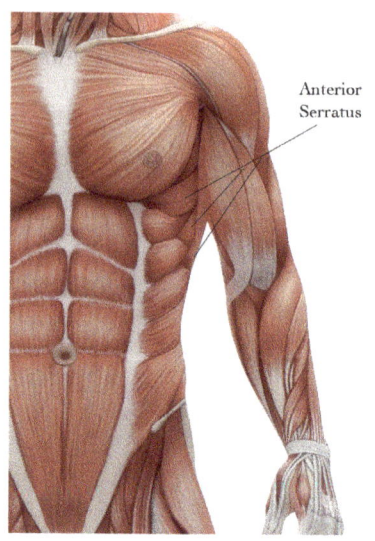

Are your income goals too low because you are undervaluing your service, or are you reaching for a goal higher than what you currently believe you can achieve? It is important to remember that you can achieve as much as your belief permits.

Are you too focused on income and not enough on service, or are you too vague when it comes to setting a financial goal? Either way, fear and doubt are the major culprits at play.

You can overcome this by evaluating your beliefs around money and personal value, and refocusing on service.

Questions to help spark your inner awareness

What ineffective beliefs do you have around money and how do they prevent you from achieving your income goals?

Do you feel deserving of what you are aiming for in life and business?

What thoughts and feelings come up when I think about my income goals?

Coracobrachialis

Yin Energy

Business: Fees, Financial Goals

Emotions: Depressed, Modesty, Regret

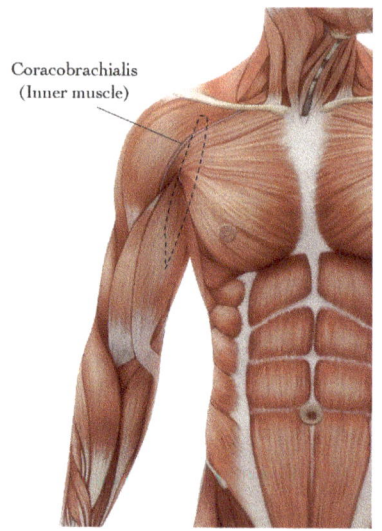

Coracobrachialis (Inner muscle)

Consider your service/product fees. When we set our fees too low, we start to resent our business and customers. When our rate is too high, we feel insufficient and end up doubting ourselves or giving too much of ourselves to compensate. The focus will be shifted from customer service to limiting beliefs, our confidence drops and the appreciation we have for ourselves starts to diminish.

You need to shift the focus back to the customer and infuse your heart into your business. Take the focus off yourself by remembering that, as a by-product of service, the business caters for all your financial needs.

All of these are equally important to the growth of your business. Ensure your financial needs are met and take good care of yourself.

Questions to help spark your inner awareness

Are you paying yourself the right wage from your business?

Are you charging enough for your products/services to not only pay yourself properly but also cover your overheads and make profit?

Deltoids

Yin Energy

Business: Income Goals, Products services

Emotions: Contempt, Regret

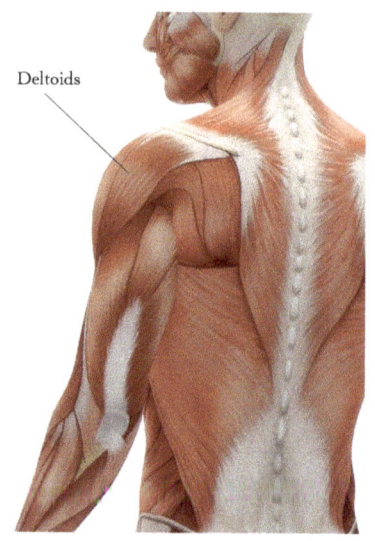

There are a couple of things to remember here. Firstly, you are currently at the right place—exactly right where you are, here and now. There is no other place you need to be. Right here, right now is 100% perfect.

Now is a good time to look back at where you have come from, what you have learnt and how much you have accomplished; be proud of yourself. Now is perfect to look at what you have achieved with your clients or products with grateful eyes. You have given a part of yourself to a world that never realised how much it needed you until you were brave enough to show up. That is exactly why you are here, to help the world.

Questions to help spark your inner awareness

Are you being too harsh on yourself for not being where you want to be or where you think your business 'should' be at this point?

Diaphragm

Yin Energy

Business: Marketing, Communications

Emotions: Depressed, Intolerance

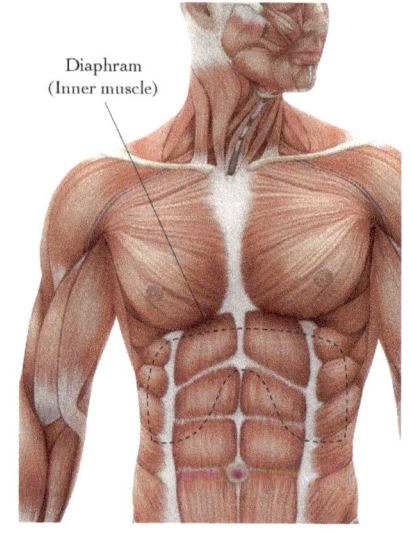

Are you starting to feel the fears arise when you speak to potential clients?

Do you tell yourself 'I am not good enough'?

Open up your voice by opening up your heart. Feel the purpose of your business within you and your work. Feel the passion in your conversations. Sales will be an automatic by-product of heartfelt conversations.

You need to work on this area when you feel or message is not being seen or heard. When you have a marketing message that look on point, but is attracting no clients.

Questions to help spark your inner awareness

Is the communication in your business free-flowing, or does it feel restricted?

Do you feel like ineffective communication between you and your clients is hindering the support required for the growth and flow of your business?

Are people reading your content?

Are you attracting sales into your business through your marketing?

Fascia Lata

Yang Energy

Business: Fees, Income Goals

Emotion: Grief, Depression, Release

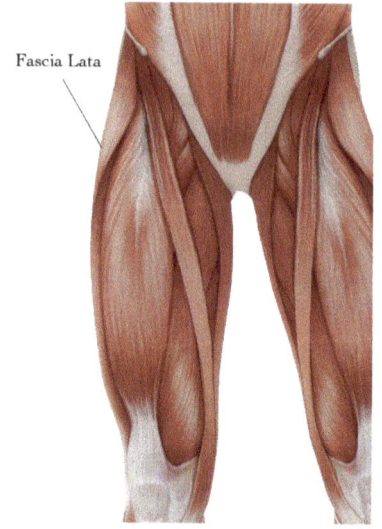

Fascia Lata

If you struggle to scale your business, you may start to feel regretful and lose your passion and faith in the future. The grief of losing our passion can set in, and the 'I am not good enough' or 'I am not worthy' self-talk can start to take over.

We need to balance the power in our legs to acquire full momentum to move forward and achieve our goals effortlessly. On the flip side, we can have too much force that it throw us off balance. This happens when we have so much power and conviction that do not originate from a heart-centred, strategic place but rather form a place of force.

Many business owners jump into working out their fees and income goals before knowing where they want to go with their business and definitely before releasing blocks and beliefs around money.

Questions to help spark your inner awareness

Is your business backed up by a passion-strategy balance that feels right?

Does your fees feel good to you?

Are you happy to tell people how much you charge?

Do you feel your fees reflect your offer?

Hamstring

Yang Energy

Business: Income Goals

Emotions: Enthusiasm, Merciful

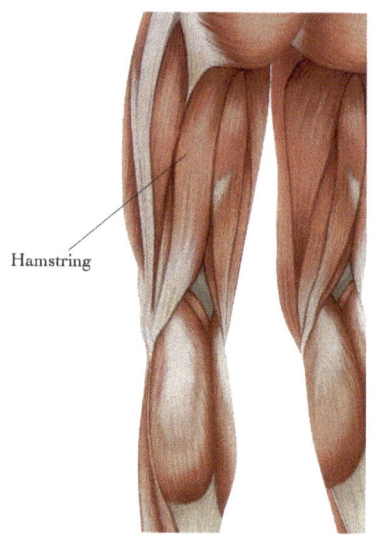

Hamstring

The 'why' is just as important as the the income goals figure itself, as it needs to be meaningful for you with full rounded energy behind it, so it becomes easy to align to.

Work out why do you need to achieve this number and how this impacts things overall.

Be agile in your approach to business strategy to achieve this goal. Know what parts of your business are thriving and what parts are not worth putting more energy, focus, nurturing into.

Be careful not to disregard things too quickly, just because they appear to be working or not on the surface. This is the time to have a look a little deeper into small tweaks that could make all the difference here.

Questions to help spark your inner awareness

Do have enough clarity about your income?

Why is your income goal the figure it is?

How does it make you feel?

Does it need to be more or less?

Quad. Lumborum

Yang Energy

Business: Client, Fees

Emotions: Release, Depression

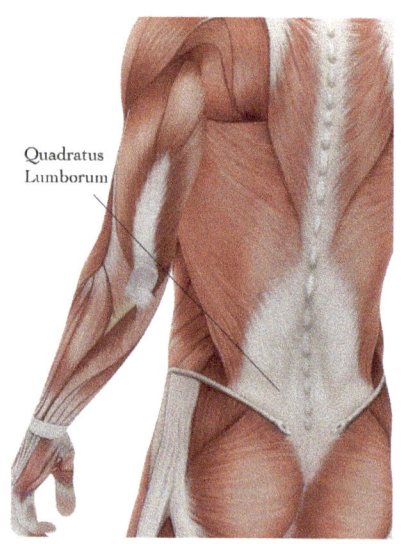

Quadratus Lumborum

It is important that your clients are in alignment with you, so that the energy flow feels free and natural.

Do you love your clients? Are they really who you want to work with? You want to work with clients you love, who also love you in return.

Ensure that the energy exchange is right, that your fees are set at the right rate—not too high and not too low for you. Place an appropriate fee on the solution you are offering your clients.

Questions to help spark your inner awareness

Is your energy exchange with your clients right?

Or

Are you giving more and taking less than you deserve?

Do they show up on time? Or cancel last minute?

If you had an abundant flow of clients, would you still work with your current list?

EVERYTHING IS ENERGY.
YOUR THOUGHTS BEGIN IT,
YOUR EMOTIONS AMPLIFIES IT,
AND YOUR ACTIONS INCREASE
THE MOMENTUM.

—UNKNOWN

FINANCES

Associated Emotions

Approval, Rejected, Assurance, Faith in the Future, Anxiety about the future, Confidence, Cynism, Sympathy, Empathy, Envy, (un) Reliable, Criticism, Contentment, Disappointment, Deprivation, Hunger|Nausea, Disgust|Doubt, Greed|Empty, Bitter

Affected Muscles

Latssimus Dosri, Mid|Low Trapezius, Opp. Pollicis Longus, Triceps, Pect. Major Clavicular, Levator Scapulae, Neck Muscles, Brachioradialis.

Pect. Major Clavicular

Yang Energy

Finances: Inherited Blocks

Emotions: Nausea, Bitter

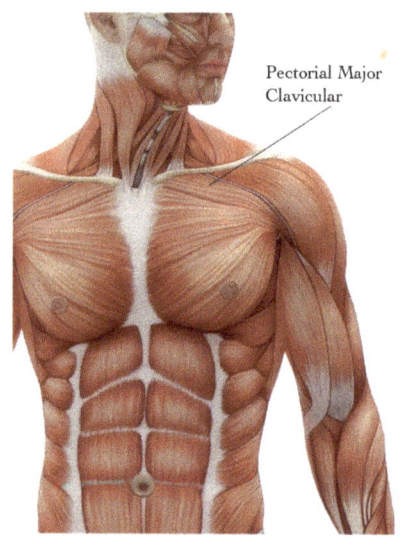

It is time to notice just how far you have come and be proud of yourself. It is time to stand up and recognise who brought you here (YOU) and all the circumstances you experienced. This includes the good times, the bad times, the rough times, the traumas, your fears and values and the beliefs passed down from parents and family. We cannot only be grateful for the wins and the triumphs. We must also be unconditionally grateful for the struggles as well. They are all part of our journey, conditioning and strength.

Now that you have recognised where you are and taken full ownership of this journey, it is time to let go of everything and take an intentional step forward. It is time to fulfil your destiny from a place of looking forward and not backward. Look ahead with immense gratitude.

There is no need to blame or to hold unwanted emotions about the past, present or what could be in the future. Know that all you have is now and make every second count.

Questions to help spark your inner awareness

Do you acknowledge how far you have come?

Are you celebrating big and small wins?

What struggles helped you get to where you are today?

How can you learn to celebrate yourself more?

Lavator Scapulae

Yang Energy

Financial: Money Blocks, Clarity around Money, Inherited blocks, Beliefs

Emotion: Bitter

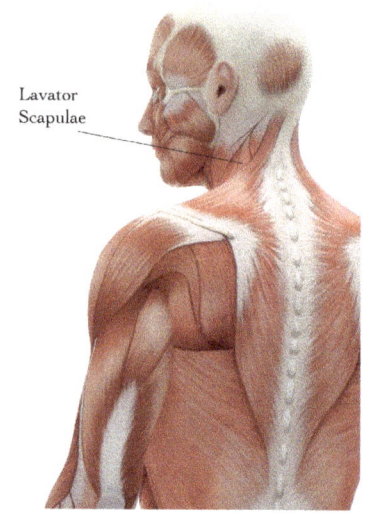

This is a good time to evaluate your fees to see whether your product/service charges are in line with both the quantity that you need to deliver and the financial goals of the business.

Questions to help spark your inner awareness

Do you believe that you can achieve this?

What self-talk goes on when you think about your finances in business?

Do you fully understand your finances in business?

Where are you currently, and where do you want/need to be financially?

What did you hear growing up about being wealthy? Was it welcomed and encouraged?

Do you feel you can fit in to a wealthy social environment?

Neck Muscles

Yang Energy

Finances: Money Blocks

Emotions: Disappointment

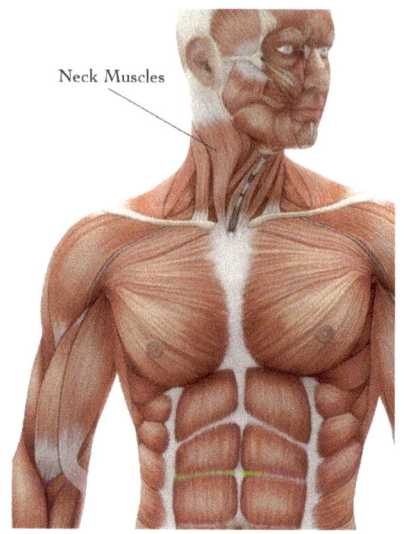

Neck Muscles

Ensure you are comfortable with how money is flowing into your business and life and you are getting your return on investment.

Questions to help spark your inner awareness

When it comes to balancing business finances, particularly around income, are you taking too many risks, or are you not taking enough risks?

Are you comfortable with the cash flow of your business, or are you too frugal?

Do you need to spend a little more to make more money (invest back into the business to give it the boost it requires)?

Brachioradialis

Yang Energy

Finances: Money Blocks

Emotions: Reliable, Hunger

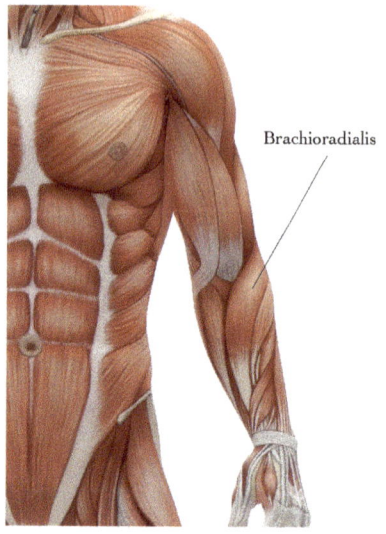

It is time to gain more knowledge and trust around your business finances. This will help you make grounded decisions in your business to assit in its growth and development.

Consider seeking advice from an external source on how to look at or manage your business finances or alternatiely making sure you are working with an accountant that you trust.

Questions to help spark your inner awareness

Are you critical about your spending habits within your business?

Would you be more satisfied with someone else overseeing the finances of your business?

Do you feel forced to spend/allocate your finances to areas that do not feel right?

Latissimus Dorsi

Ying Energy

Finances: Personal Goals, Money Blocks & Beliefs

Emotion: Assurance & Confidence

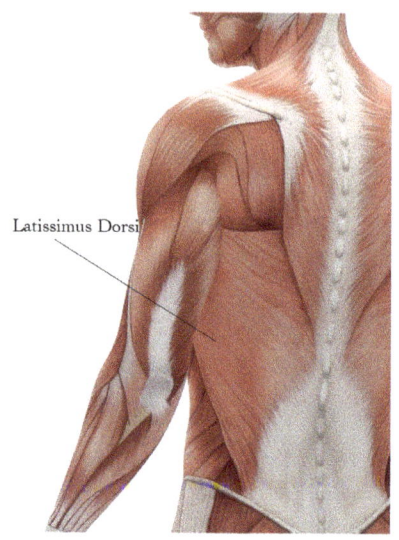

The energy behind your figures is meaningless without clarity. Be clear about your financial goals. You should know what you need to grow and scale your business, as well as the actions needed. Have a clear goal on how much you need to take from your business for personal expenses (wages).

Questions to help spark your inner awareness

Are you making too many guesses about your figures?

Are you being too soft on yourself and nurturing the 'small play' mentality?

Are you holding back from playing a bigger business game, and is this preventing you from reaching your financial goals?

Mid/Lower Trapezius

Yin Energy

Finances: Personal goals, Inherited Blocks

Emotions: Faith of the Future, Cynicism

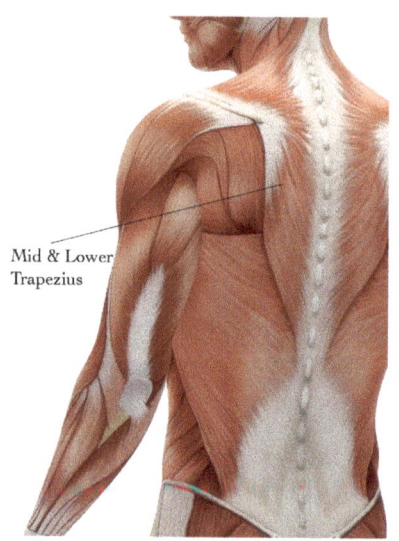

Mid & Lower Trapezius

This involves attempting to do too much or doing too little for the growth of your business. Have a look into taking external opinions as gospel and not giving it the thought that you need before taking action, or are you resistance to knowledge which facilitates change and growth.

Take note of your self-talk, beliefs and actions as they may be toxic elements that no longer serve you.

It is time to cut out the external noise and align yourself to your business. This way you will know who to connect with on what and you will also raise awearness around what inner voice needs to be healed.

Questions to help spark your inner awareness

Are you afraid of showing the real you, and do you show a cleaner, more polished version of yourself?

Are you hiding the real you for fear of being criticised?

Do you need to take action to embark on a more authentic aligned business journey?

Opponens Pollicis Longus

Yin Energy

Finances: Personal Goals, Money Blocks

Emotions: Faith in the Future, Anxiety for the future, Envy

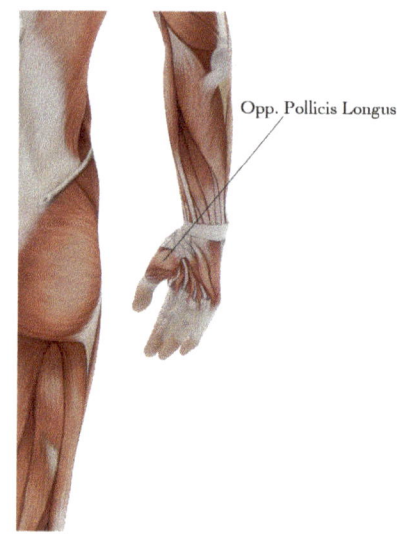

Holding on too tight to financial beliefs that do not serve you makes your daily business life harder than it should be. However, also consider this: Are you not holding on tightly enough? You may be stuck in awe of others' success while neglecting yours. Do you feel that what others have is out of your reach? Consider beliefs like 'I do not deserve…', 'I am not good enough'.

Questions to help spark your inner awareness

Are your beliefs around work and money the same as your parents'?

Can you see the same pattern of beliefs playing out in your life?

Triceps

Yin Energy

Finances: Money Beliefs

Emotions: Cynicism, Sympathy, Envy

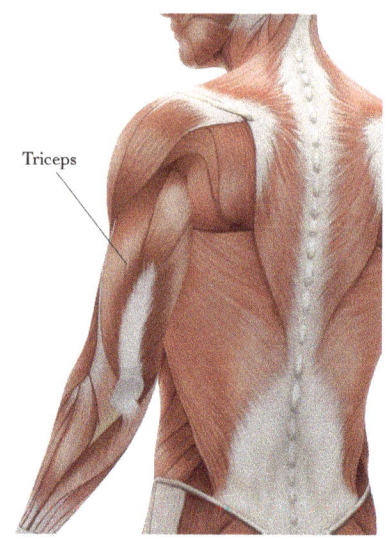

Triceps

This will reflect as being envious of what others have and what their finances have brought into their life. It is time to reassess your beliefs around finances. You may need guidance in this aspect to ensure you are comfortable and content with setting and achieving the budget for your business and your personal life.

It is time to step down from a high-level view and break things down into finer details.

Questions to help spark your inner awareness

Are you too consumed in other people's thoughts and not making up your own beliefs that work for you?

What beliefs are triggered when I look around and see what others have?

Do I feel worthy? Do I believe I can do it?

Is what they have, what I want or does it just appear nice from the outside, but what you want is very different?

YOUR TIME IS LIMITED, SO DON'T
WASTE IT LIVING SOMEONE ELSE'S LIFE.
DON'T BE TRAPPED BY DOGMA—
WHICH IS LIVING WITH THE RESULTS
OF OTHER PEOPLE'S THINKING.
DON'T LET THE NOISE OF OTHERS'
OPINIONS DROWN OUT YOUR
INNER VOICE.
AND MOST IMPORTANTLY, HAVE THE
COURAGE TO FOLLOW YOUR HEART
AND INTUITION.

—STEVE JOBS

PERSONAL

Associated Emotions

Love, Anger, Rage, Wrath, Self Righteous, Indignation, Forbearance, Assertive, Helpless, Passive, Humble, Proud, Choice, Wrath, Distressed, Transformation, Unhappiness, Resentment, Happiness, Content.

Affected Muscle

Anterior Deltoid, Popliteus, Pect. Major Sternal, Rhomboids

Anterior Deltoid

Yang Energy

Personal: Purpose, Spirituality

Emotions: Helpless, Passive, Humble, Proud, Choice

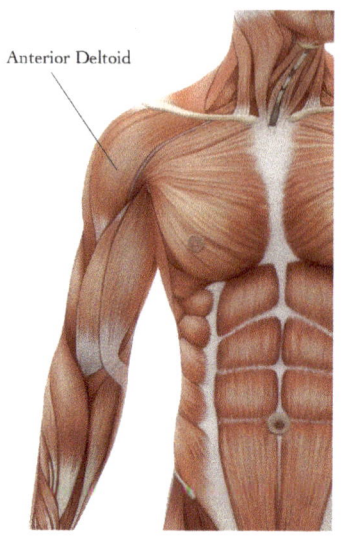

Anterior Deltoid

It is time to look at your self-care routine. Self-care relative to the Anterior Deltoid focuses on actions that guarantee mental stability. When things feel hard, you have to relieve the pressure. Life can feel overwhelming when there is stagnant energy. You may need to consult professional help to release this pressure, that is, contractors, freelancers, healers, coaches, etc.

Questions to help spark your inner awareness

Are you taking time out for you?

Are you giving too much of your energy away?

Popliteus

Yang Energy

Personal: Love, Self Confidence

Emotions: Love, Anger, Rage, Self-Righteous, Assertive, Helpless.

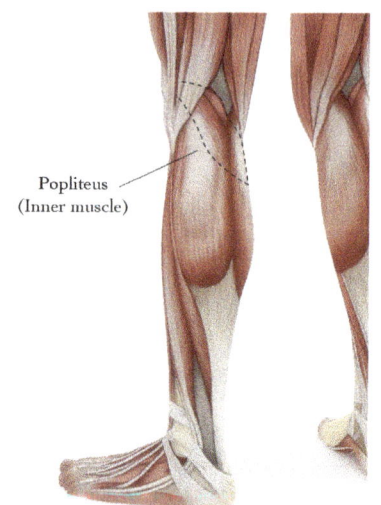

Popliteus (Inner muscle)

This is a feeling of self-doubt that keeps you on the same spot. You may feel like you are moving in circles with no actual progress. These things may seem small, but they make a huge impact on your life due to inaction and can accumulate to a feeling of overwhelm.

By writing down a list of the little things in life and gradually addressing each of them, you will find the energy to rebalance and regain your confidence. Trust and believe that you can achieve one task at a time, and you will see how quickly you move forward. Take time out to reset your energy in between tasks and ask for guidance when you need to, either from the universe, your team or a mentor.

Questions to help spark your inner awareness

Do you feel stagnant in life?

What are the little things in life hindering you from moving forward?

What have I created in my life that I am greatful for?

Pect Major Sternal

Ying Energy

Personal: Fear, Limiting beliefs, Purpose

Emotions: Distress

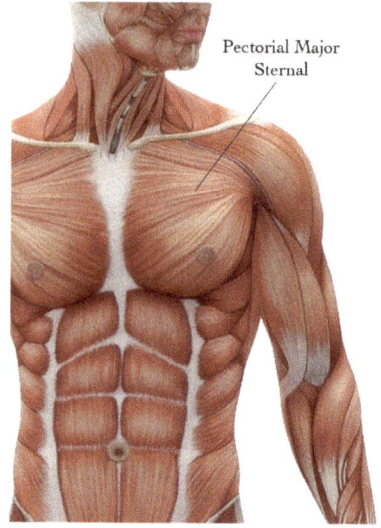

Are you exhibiting outward calmness while being internally distressed because you know you are capable of achieving more but do not know how to reach it?

It is time to work out two things: What do you believe about yourself or your work that is holding you back and hindering your ability to serve? Do you need to further define your purpose?

Be conscious of the toxic and negative thoughts you say to yourself about what you want to do in life. It will give you clue of where to begin your healing and letting go.

Questions to help spark your inner awareness

Are there things in your life that you are finding toxic and overwhelming?

Do you feel off purpose?

Are you holding on to beliefs that are clouding your sense of purpose?

Do you feel lost at times?

Rhomboids

Yin Energy

Personal: Purpose

Emotions: Resentment, Content

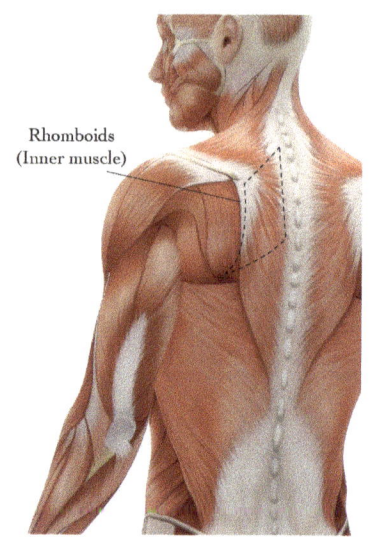

This is about supporting ourselves and trusting that we are taking action based on our internal guidance. Are you paying too much attention to your toxic self-talk or people telling you that you are wrong, cannot do it or are not good enough?

This muscle can be over energised and give you problems when you ignore the direction of your purpose.

Questions to help spark your inner awareness

Are you listening to toxic self-doubt or self-talk?

What is that talk? Feel into it and let it go.

THE MOMENT YOU CHANGE
YOUR PERCEPTION,
IS THE MOMENT YOU REWRITE
THE CHEMISTRY OF YOUR BODY.

—DR. BRUCE LIPTON

HEALTH

Associated Emotions

Peace, Dread, Panic, Terror, Restlessness, Frustration, Inner direction, Impatience, Confidence, Courage, Fear, Anxiety, Sexual (in)Security, Creative (in)Security, Cautious, Reckless, Careless, (in)Devisive, (un)Loyal

Affected Muscles

Peroneus, Sacrospinalis, Tibials, Psoas, Upper Trapezius, Iliacus

Sacrospialis

Yang Energy

Health: Mental Clarity

Emotions: Confidence

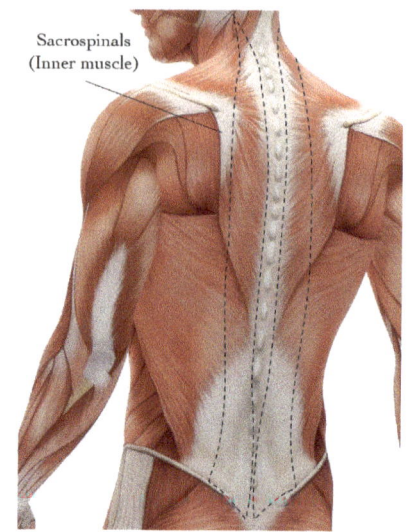

This muscles can play up when you neglect yourself. This may include a string of self-care rituals that need to be evaluated and refined, or even to start to put sometime in place.

Self care rituals around mental clarity is about giving the mind space to process daily throughts. This could be meditations, journaling, talk therapy. Anything that helps clear your mind.

When we clear our mind, we give space for processing the things that are throwing us off balance.

Questions to help spark your inner awareness

What small things in your business annoy you and is throwing you off balance?

Are you paying too much or too little attention to one aspect of your business or life?

What do you need to tweak in your self-care rituals to boost your confidence and mental clarity?

What have you been avoiding doing, or what have you done too much of that is contributing to not having the mental clarity that you need?

Tibials

Yang Energy

Health: Mental Clarity

Emotions: Frustration, Terror, Restlessness, Impatience, Courage

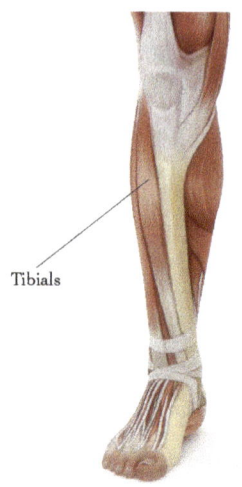
Tibials

Questions to help spark your inner awareness

When thrown off balance, do you recover quickly?

When you are criticised or judged, do you take it to heart and start to second-guess yourself? Do you fight or learn from the situation and move forward with even more clarity and ease?

Do you need to let go of aspects of your business that prevent you from moving forward? Are you running an effective strategy in your business, or are you spraying and praying for results?

Are you struggling to maintain your love for your business? Is the love flowing and translating into sales and growth?

Psoas

Yin Energy

Health: Physical Health

Emotions: Indecisiveness

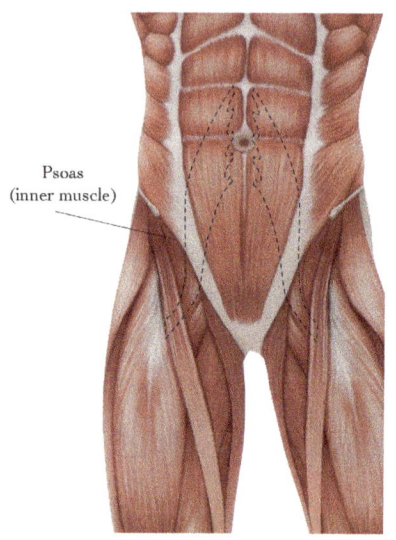

Psoas (inner muscle)

Are you looking after your phsycial body? If you take care of your physical body, you will make better decisions within your business and make massive progress.

Questions to help spark your inner awareness

Physically, what do you need to support your business?

Do you need to be more active and utilize more oxygen to restore physical and mental balance?

Is there an aspect of your health that you are not prioritising even though you know that more effort is required in that aspect?

Upper Trapezius

Yin Energy

Health: Mind-body Connection

Emotions: Recklessness

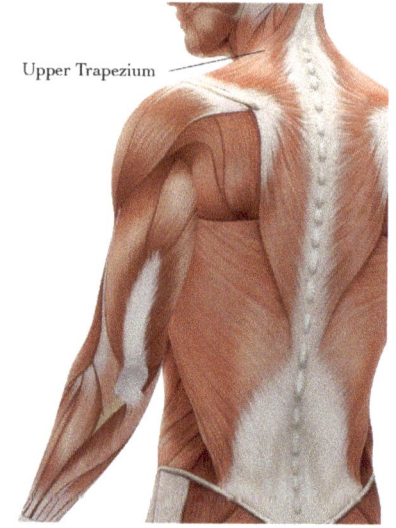

You are filtering through ideas that point 25% in the right direction of your goal. Ensure you do not go off track with shiny object syndrome or do a task that is not relevant to your goal.

Look at this from a business strategy and a personal health perspective. Do you know where you are headed, so that your strategy, goals, boundaries, values and ideas have something to align to? Could you refine the vision of your current goal?

Questions to help spark your inner awareness

Are you making hasty decisions?

Do you find yourself too often making decisions that after feels like the wrong decision?

Iliacus

Yin Energy

Health: Mind-body Connection

Emotions: Sexual (in) Security, Careless, (un) Loyal

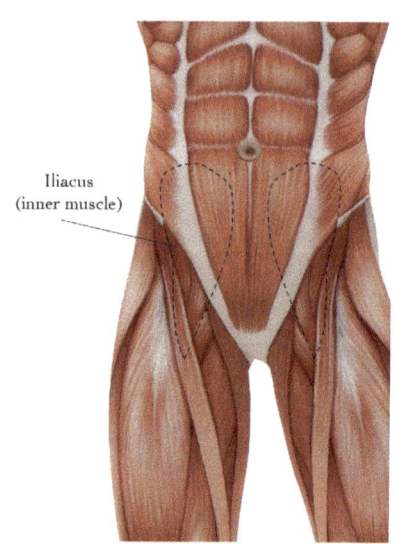

You reside more in your physical headspace than your heart space. It is easier to be you and stand out than being something that you are not. Work from a place of inner knowing and understanding that is aligned to your journey in life and business.

Are you pushing things that need to be done aside, or are you pushing yourself aside and not giving yourself due credit?

Either way, you are not seeing the full picture as your head is too crowed.

Questions to help spark your inner awareness

Do you make decisions from the head or the heart?

Are you overly strategic in your ideas and decisions?

Peroneus

Yang Energy

Health: Mental Clarity, Mind-body Connection

Emotions: Courage, Inner direction

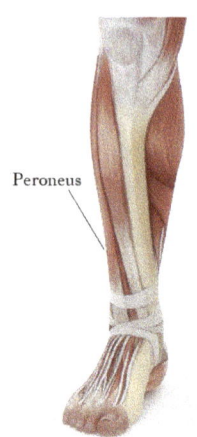

When we move forward hesitantly or with too much haste, we miss the internal guiding messages that tell us 'how' to move forward.

When this is over energised, we may walk through life destructively with an unstoppable force which may feel hard, overwhelming and even reckless.

Sit in a place of peace. Flow will help balance this muscle.

Questions to help spark your inner awareness

Are you walking courageously in your direction, or are you treading with so much caution or even heading in a direction that does not truly light you up?

Do you feel grounded and strongly guided from within, or are you second-guessing every step that you take?

Many of us do not realise our true potential and settle for our current lifestyle. Are you ready to dream a little bigger and reach a little further to turn your dreams into reality?

PART 3

Support

Tools and Resources

It takes a great deal of self-awareness to fully embody new change in your life. Self-awareness to see what needs to change and then to create the change you want to see in yourself and your life. This will create lasting change from your current thoughts, habits and actions into new rituals that support our desired lifestyle.

Please, keep this in mind when making any shift in your life, especially when shifting from unconscious paradigms to a new awareness, and doing the healing work that goes with it all, that you should give yourself the support, nurturing and space required to not only make the changes but for them to fully integrate within you. Go gentle on yourself and don't expect all changes to happen at once, but to slowly create lasting change in your life.

Keep learning and growing, will be your key to continued growth.

On my website and social platforms, I continually bring our new tips, tools, interviews, and much more information and courses to help you create the change that you want in your life. As well as offering you private consultations to guide and support you on your journey forward.

www.jennifermccormack.com.au

Instagram – @Jennifermccormackwellness

Tiktok – Jennifermccwellness

Youtube – Jennifer McCormack

Facebook – @jennifermccormackwellness

Conclusion

It is so important to remember that you have the power of the universe within you, and no matter where you are starting from, and no matter how you are feeling right now, you CAN have, do and be ANYTHING you want. You are a perfect gift to this world and just being here is enough. As an entrepreneur, I can feel your yearning to reach your greatness and spread your light to the world—you will. Sometimes, we just need to get to know ourselves a little deeper. I hope this book empowers you to fill up your OWN cup, travel your OWN path and be your OWN magnificent person.

During any journey of healing and self-discovery, you will peel back layers that you did not realise that were there, to reveal parts of yourself that will make you laugh, cry and be immensely proud.

Your mind, body and soul are in continuous communication with you, mentally and physically. You now know not be too hard on yourself when you feel disconnected. Love exactly where you are and move forward from there by asking yourself one simple question: 'How do I feel?' This is the most powerful tool that you can take throughout your life. It is the window to self-awareness, and from this point, you can use this book to help you navigate back to where you want to be.

As a business owner, you are a beacon of light for your staff, your customers and the world. You have a gift the world needs. We give people the product and service we create as well as the power and intention we create it with.

This is why I wrote this book, to empower you and the entrepreneur within you to spread the love and this message to your customers and your community so that they receive the gift of awareness required to harness their true power.

You are a beautiful being with great intentions and extraordinary power. Go forth and create with strength, power and love. Know that you are fully supported by yourself, the universe and me.

Acknowledgements

First and foremost to Darcy Smyth, who planted the seed for this book in my mind. I would have never thought of writing a book until you mentioned it to me. I was excited about the idea from the start.

To Emily Gowor, who was often more excited about this book than I was. Her infectious enthusiasm was all I needed to keep me going when I got writer's block. Your guidance and mentorship made it easy for me to pull this information together and write it down for the world to read. I have never come across a human with the zest for life and the passion for their work as you do.

To Helen Lloyd, my spiritual mentor, who has been pushing me to finish this book, always reminding me of how important it is to write. You have a heart of gold, and as you say, with a sledgehammer that was necessary at times. I am so grateful for your persistence with me as I grew and journeyed with this book. You reminded me how this book was as much for me as it was for others—a huge healing journey. You made me aware of my true strength, that I am capable of doing work like this.

To my boys, Lachlan and Liam, who at the time of writing this book are ten and seven years old. You have inspired me to live up to the fullness of my being. You have been my reason for growing and learning, not only to be the best version of myself but to be an inspiration to you. If there is anything I would like to gift you as a mother, it is that you learn to live life from your authentic self and to follow your bliss. I love you with all of my heart.

About The Author

Jennifer McCormack is a Kinesiologist, author and speaker. She works with Coaches, Healers, CEOs and entrepreneurs from around the globe within her private practice, helping them understand how their emotions affect their physical body and their current reality and facilitating their healing and personal growth process.

After years of struggling with with food intolerances, depression, anxiety, PND and multiple miscarriages as well as struggling to grow her private practice, Jennifer realised all her problems were interconnected in some way. As she journeyed through the healing process with her emotions and body, the business automatically expanded, and opportunities flowed in.

Originally trained as a Fashion Designer, Jennifer's career change began after the successful delivery of her first son. She wanted to leave the stressful life of corporate codependancy behind and raise a family in a more holistic environment. Jennifer is now a trained SFEF Kinesiologist, NLP (Neuro-Linguistic Programming), NRT (Neuro Reprocessing Therapy) and Reiki Practitioner and Hypnotherapist. Jennifer is dedicated to helping people heal and reconnect with the depth of who they are, to enable them grow to an elite level in life and business.

Jennifer currently works in her private practice seeing clients, as well as speaking and facilitating online courses to help inspire people to take those extra steps forward in looking after themselves and creating the future that they want and deserve.

Jennifer inspires people to create that butterfly effect within their communities, to help spread the word that you can feel good and have want you want.

INDEX

Emotions

(in)decisive 221, 226

(in)tolerance 176, 178, 184

(un)loyal 221, 230

(un)Merciful 176, 188

(un)reliable 192, 200

Anger 150, 168

Anger 211, 214

Anxiety 221

Anxiety re. future 192, 206

Apathy 176

Appreciated 150, 172

Approved 192

Assertive 211, 214

Assimilation 150

Assurance 192, 202

Balance 150, 160, 164, 174

Bitter 192

Calm 150

Careless 221, 230

Cautious 221

Cheerful 176

Choice 211, 212

Clarity 192, 202

Confidence 192, 202

Confidence 221, 222

Contempt 176, 182

Content 211, 218

Contentment 192

Courage 221, 224, 232

Creative (in)Security 221

Criticism 192

Cynicism 192, 204, 208

Depression 176, 180, 184, 186, 190

Deprivation 192

Despair 150

Despondent 150, 162

Disappointment 192, 198

Disgust 192

Distain 176

Distance

Distressed 211, 216

Doubt 192

Dread 221

Elation 150, 160, 164

Embrassement 145, 146

Empathy 192

Empty 192

Enthusiasm 176, 188

Envy 192, 206, 208

Faith in the future 192, 204, 206

False Pride 176

Fear 221

Forbearance 211

Forgiveness 150

Frustration 221, 224
Gloomy 150, 152, 154, 156
Greed 192
Grief 176, 186
Guilt 176
Happiness 211
Hate 150
Haughty 176
Heaviness 150, 164
Helpless 211, 212, 214
Honesty 145, 146
Hope(less) 150, 160, 162
Humble 211, 212
Humiliated 150
Humility 176
Hunger 192, 200
Hysteria 150, 152, 156
Impatience 221, 224
Indifference 176
Indignation 211
Inner Direction 221, 232
Insecure 150
Internalization 150, 172
Jealousy 150, 152, 154, 158

Joy 150
Letting go 176
Lightness 150, 160, 166
Loneliness 150, 166
Love 150, 168
Love 211, 214
Modesty 176, 178, 180
Nausea 192, 194
Nourishing 150, 170, 172
Over-excited 150
Overwhelem 145, 148
Panic 221
Passive 211, 212
Peace 221
Prejudice 176
Proud 211, 212
Rage 211, 214
Reckless 221, 228
Regret 176, 178, 180, 182
Rejected 192
Relaxation 150
Release 176, 186, 190
Remorse 150
Resentment 211, 218
Responsibility 150, 154, 156

Restlessness 221, 224
Sadness 150, 170
Scorn 176
Secure 150
Self – Respect 145, 148
Self Righteous 211, 214
Self-esteem 150
Self-worth 150, 168, 176
Serving 150
Sexual (in)security 221, 230
Shame 145, 148
Shyness 145, 148
Sorrow 150
Stubbornness 150
Success 145, 148
Supported 145, 146
Sympathy 192, 208
Terror 221, 224
Tranquillity 150, 152, 154
Transformation 211
Truth 145, 146
Unappreciated 150, 172
Unhappiness 211
Unsupported 145, 146
Wrath 211

Index

Muscles

Abdominals 150, 172
Adductors 150, 154
Anterior Deltoid 211, 212
Anterior Serratus 176, 178
Brachioradialis 193, 200
Coracobrachialis 176, 180
Deltoids 176, 182
Diaphragm 176, 184
Fascia Lata 176, 186
Gastrocnemius 150, 166
Gluteus Madius 150, 152
Gluteus Maximus 150, 158
Gracilis 150, 162
Hamstring 176, 188
Iliacus 221, 230
Latissimus Dorsi 193, 202
Lavator Scapulae 193, 196
Mid/Lower Trapezius 193, 204
Neck Muscles 193, 198
Opponens Pollicis Longus 193, 206
Pect. Major Clavicular 193, 194
Pect. Major Sternal 211, 216
Peroneus 221, 232
Piriformis 150, 156
Popliteus 211, 214
Psoas 221, 226
Quad. Lumborum 176, 190
Quadriceps 150, 170
Rhomboids 211, 218
Sacrospialis 221, 222
Sartorius 150, 174
Soleus 150, 164
Subscapularis 150, 168
Supraspinatus 145, 148
Teres Major 145, 146
Teres Minor 150, 160
Tibials 221, 224
Triceps 193, 208
Upper Trapezius 221, 228

www.ingramcontent.com/pod-product-compliance
Lightning Source LLC
Chambersburg PA
CBHW051535010526
44107CB00064B/2736